BUILDING BASIC VOCABULARY B

Robert J. Marzano

Australia • Brazil • Japan • Korea • Mexico • Singapore • Spain • United Kingdom • United States

Building Basic Vocabulary B
Robert J. Marzano

Publisher: Sherrise Roehr

Executive Editor: Carmela Fazzino-Farah

Managing Editor: Kellie Cardone

Development Editors: Cécile Engeln and
Marissa Petrarca

Senior Product Manager: Barbara
Quincer Coulter

Associate Marketing Manager: Jennifer
Ellegood

Director of Content and Media Production:
Michael Burggren

Senior Content Project Manager: Daisy Sosa

Manufacturing Manager: Marcia Locke

Manufacturing Buyer: Marybeth Hennebury

Cover Design: Page 2 LLC

Interior Design: Muse Group, Inc.

Composition: PreMediaGlobal

Contributing Writers: Karen Haller Beer,
Jackie Counts, and Wendy Criner

ISBN-13: 978-1-133-30850-8

ISBN-10: 1-133-30850-3

National Geographic Learning
20 Channel Center St.
Boston, MA 02210
USA

Cengage Learning is a leading provider of customized learning solutions with
office locations around the globe, including Singapore, the United Kingdom,
Australia, Mexico, Brazil, and Japan. Locate your local office at:
international.cengage.com/region

Cengage Learning products are represented in Canada by Nelson Education, Ltd.

Visit National Geographic Learning online at **ngl.cengage.com**
Visit our corporate website at **www.cengage.com**

Printed in the United States of America
1 2 3 4 5 6 7 16 15 14 13 12

REVIEWERS

Renee M. Belvis
Dunedin Highland Middle
School
Dunedin, FL

Brian Cerda
Sabina Magnet School
Chicago, IL

Ashley Cimo
Amos Alonzo Stagg High
School
Palos Hills, IL

Fred Cochran
Lincoln Unified School District
Stockton, CA

Raquel Cruz
Country Club Middle School
Miami, FL

Meg Daniewicz
New Millennium Academy
Minneapolis, MN

Amber Driscoll
March Middle School
Moreno Valley, CA

Annie Duong
San Joaquin COE
Stockton, CA

Jill Hoffmann
Victor J. Andrew High School
Tinley Park, IL

Laura Hook
Howard County Public School
System
Ellicott City, MD

Tara Kim
March Middle School
Moreno Valley, CA

Alice Kos
Minneapolis Public Schools
Minneapolis, MN

Elizabeth Koutny
Ames Middle School
Berwyn, IL

Mary Lein
Rochester ISD
Rochester, MN

Sam Nofziger
The English Learner Group
Fresno, CA

Esmeralda Placencia
Chicago Public Schools
Chicago, IL

Maria Rivera
Richard Edwards Elementary
School
Chicago, IL

Mytzy Rodriguez-Kufner
Round Lake Area Schools
Round Lake, IL

Nathalie Rumowicz
Seminole Middle School
Plantation, FL

Susan Sharko
Old Quarry Middle School
Lemont, IL

Dr. LaWanna Shelton
Trevecca Nazarene University
Nashville, TN

Gwen Snow
Jefferson County Public Schools –
ESL Newcomer Academy
Louisville, KY

Claudia Viloria
South Ft. Myers High School
Ft. Myers, FL

Brenda Ward
Lafayette School Corporation
Lafayette, IN

Bryn Watson
Hough Street Elementary
School
Barrington, IL

Jennifer White
ESOL Program, Charleston
County School District
Charleston, SC

Vicki Writsel
Bowling Green Independent
Schools
Bowling Green, KY

CONTENTS

Book A Super Clusters

Book B Super Clusters

Book C Super Clusters

Note: This Contents section provides information on how to find the first instance of each super cluster. For information on where specific clusters can be found, please refer to the Appendix on pages 288 to 291.

87. Locations Near Water

Check (✔) the words you already know. Then, listen and repeat.

 Tracks 1–4

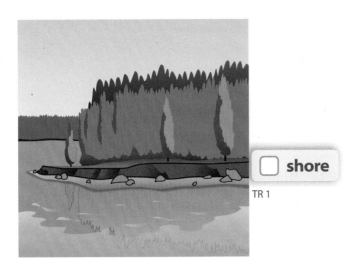

☐ **shore**
TR 1

Definitions

A **beach** is an area of sand or stones next to a lake or ocean.

The **coast** is the land that is next to the ocean.

An **island** is a piece of land that is completely surrounded by water.

The **shore** of an ocean or a lake is the land along the edge of it.

☐ **coast**
TR 3

☐ **island**
TR 2

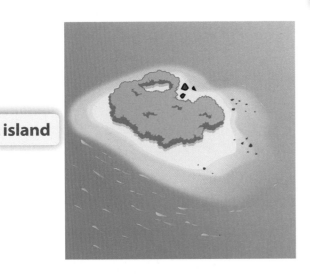

☐ **beach**
TR 4

1

Check Your Understanding

A. Write **T** for **true statements** and **F** for **false statements**.

1. _____ A beach is an area of sand next to a mountain.

2. _____ The land next to the ocean is called the coast.

3. _____ An island is completely surrounded by water.

4. _____ You can't see water if you are standing on the shore.

B. Underline the correct word to complete each sentence.

1. We walked along the (**island** / **shore**) of Lake Sabrina and looked for a place to fish.

2. Steven and Rachel want to go on vacation on a tropical (**island** / **coast**) such as Fiji or Hawaii.

3. Denise spent the day at the (**beach** / **island**) and watched the surfers.

4. They took a drive along the (**coast** / **island**) to see beautiful views of the ocean.

Challenge Words

Check (✔) the words you already know.

☐ lakeside ☐ peninsula ☐ riverbank ☐ seashore

☐ mainland ☐ pier ☐ riverside ☐ shoreline

101. Forms of Water / Liquid

Check (✔) the words you already know. Then, listen and repeat.

 Tracks 1–13

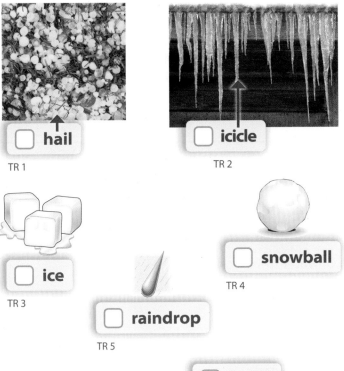

☐ **hail**
TR 1

☐ **icicle**
TR 2

☐ **ice**
TR 3

☐ **raindrop**
TR 5

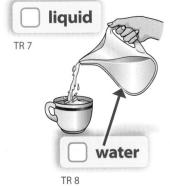

☐ **snowball**
TR 4

☐ **liquid**
TR 7

☐ **water**
TR 8

☐ **snow**
TR 6

Definitions

Hail is rain that freezes and falls to the ground as small balls of ice.

Ice is frozen water.

An **icicle** is a pointed piece of ice. **Icicles** are formed by water that freezes as it falls in small drops.

A **liquid** is a substance that is not a solid or a gas. **Liquids** flow and can be poured. Water and oil are **liquids**.

Rain is water that falls from the clouds in small drops.

A **rainbow** is a curve of bright colors that you can sometimes see in the sky after it rains.

A **raindrop** is a single drop of water from a cloud.

Rainfall is the amount of rain that falls in a place during a particular period.

Snow is white flakes formed from frozen water that falls from the sky in cold weather.

A **snowball** is a ball of snow formed with the hands.

(continued)

☐ **rain**
TR 9

☐ **rainfall**
TR 10

☐ **rainbow**
TR 11

3

snowman

TR 12

steam

TR 13

Definitions

A **snowman** is a large shape of a person that is made out of snow.

Steam is the gas in the air that forms when water is heated.

Water is a colorless liquid that falls from the sky when it rains. **Water** is used for drinking and washing. Everyone needs **water** to live.

Check Your Understanding

A. Match each word to the correct description. One description will not be used.

1. _____ ice
2. _____ rain
3. _____ snow
4. _____ liquid
5. _____ rainbow
6. _____ raindrop
7. _____ rainfall
8. _____ snowball
9. _____ snowman
10. _____ steam
11. _____ icicle
12. _____ water
13. _____ hail

a. a single drop of water from a cloud

b. hot gas from heated water

c. a pointed piece of ice

d. not a solid and not a gas

e. water falling from the clouds

f. a colorless liquid people need to live

g. frozen white flakes that fall from the sky

h. curved shape of bright colors in the sky

i. shape of a person made of snow

j. amount of rain at a particular time and place

k. frozen water

l. small balls of ice that fall to the ground

m. a very light rain

n. a ball of snow

B. Circle the word in each group that does not belong.

1. raindrop   liquid   ice   rain

2. snowball   rainbow   snowman   snow

3. steam   snow   ice   snowball

4. ice   icicle   hail   rainfall

5. water   rain   liquid   rainfall

Challenge Words

Check (✔) the words you already know.

☐ drizzle   ☐ frost   ☐ iceberg   ☐ precipitation

☐ fluid   ☐ glacier   ☐ mist   ☐ vapor

102. Bodies of Water

Check (✔) the words you already know. Then, listen and repeat.

Tracks 1–9

☐ lake

TR 1

☐ pond

TR 2

☐ puddle

TR 3

☐ river

TR 4

Check Your Understanding

A. Underline the correct word to complete each sentence.

1. There are a lot of sailboats on the (**lake / puddle**) today.

2. The motorboat cruised around the (**creek / bay**).

3. Carl stepped in every (**puddle / pond**) on the sidewalk.

4. Whales and dolphins live in the (**ocean / stream**).

5. The water in this (**pond / river**) flows out to the ocean.

6. Tom walked along the (**sea / creek**) in the forest.

7. Sandy enjoyed fishing in the (**stream / puddle**).

8. We sat near the small (**ocean / pond**) and watched the ducks swim.

9. The (**sea / puddle**) was full of seabirds feeding on the fish.

creek
stream

TR 5 and TR 6

Atlantic Ocean

ocean

TR 7

Mediterranean Sea

sea

TR 8

bay

TR 9

Definitions

A **bay** is a large body of water around which the land forms a curve.

A **creek** is a stream or a small river.

A **lake** is a large body of fresh water with land around it.

The **ocean** is the very large body of salt water that covers much of the Earth's surface.

A **pond** is a body of water smaller than a lake.

A **puddle** is a small, temporary pool of water.

A **river** is a body of water that flows in one direction between two river banks.

A **sea** is a body of salt water that is part of an ocean or is surrounded by land.

A **stream** is a small, narrow river.

B. Match each word to the correct description. One description will not be used.

1. _____ lake
2. _____ ocean
3. _____ puddle
4. _____ river
5. _____ sea
6. _____ stream
7. _____ bay
8. _____ creek
9. _____ pond

a. area of land soaked with water

b. large area of salt water that is part of an ocean

c. large area of water with land around it

d. small pool of water on the ground

e. salt water that covers much of the Earth's surface

f. stream or small river

g. body of water around which the coastline bends

h. small, narrow river

i. long line of water that flows in one direction

j. small area of water

Challenge Words

Check (✔) the words you already know.

☐ brook   ☐ delta   ☐ marsh   ☐ swamp   ☐ waterfall

☐ current   ☐ lagoon   ☐ rapids   ☐ tide

127. Water / Liquid (Related Actions)

Check (✔) the words you already know. Then, listen and repeat.

Tracks 1–25

☐ dive
TR 2

☐ drip
TR 4

☐ drain
TR 3

☐ boil
TR 1

☐ melt
TR 7

☐ pour
TR 12

☐ float
TR 10

☐ spill
TR 11

☐ sink
TR 16

☐ wet
TR 17

☐ splash
TR 18

☐ stir
TR 21

☐ swim
TR 22

☐ bubble
TR 23

Definitions

When a hot liquid **boils**, bubbles appear in it and it starts to change into steam.

When a liquid **bubbles**, bubbles move in it, for example, because it is boiling.

If you **dive** into water, you jump in so that your arms and your head go in first.

If you **drain** a liquid, you remove it by making it flow somewhere else.

When liquid **drips**, it falls in drops.

If a liquid **dribbles**, it flows in a thin stream.

If something **floats**, it stays on the surface of a liquid and does not sink.

If you **flush** something, you clean it with water.

If a liquid **freezes**, it becomes solid because the temperature is low.

If a container **leaks**, there is a hole in it that lets liquid or gas escape.

When a solid substance **melts**, it changes to a liquid because it has become warm.

If you **pour** a liquid or other substance, you make it flow out of a container.

If a boat **sinks**, it goes below the surface of the water.

If something is **slippery** or **slick**, it is smooth or wet and is difficult to walk on or to hold.

If you **soak** something, you put it into liquid for a long time.

If you **spill** a liquid, you accidentally make it flow from its container.

If you **splash** in water, you hit the water in a noisy way.

If you **spray** a liquid somewhere, drops of the liquid cover a place.

If you **sprinkle** something with a liquid or powder, you drop a little of it over the surface.

If you **squirt** a liquid somewhere, it comes out of a narrow opening very quickly.

If you **stir** a liquid, you mix it in a circular motion, sometimes using a spoon.

When you **swim**, you move through water by making movements with your arms and legs.

When a liquid **trickles**, a small amount of it flows slowly.

If something is **wet**, it is covered in liquid.

Check Your Understanding

A. Circle the word that best matches the meaning of the bold words.

1. The rain is **falling in drops** from the roof.

    a. pouring   b. dripping   c. splashing

2. Look at the duck **staying on the surface and not sinking** in the pond.

    a. diving   b. freezing   c. floating

3. All of the ice in my lemonade **changed to water because it is hot outside.**

    a. melted   b. drained   c. froze

4. Please **put** the juice in the pitcher into these cups.

    a. spill   b. pour   c. dribble

5. We need to **remove the water from** the pool **and make it flow elsewhere.**

    a. drain   b. drip   c. splash

6. Jenna was too scared to **jump head-first** into the pool.

    a. sink   b. dive   c. float

7. Don't **hit the water at** me!

    a. splash   b. wet   c. spray

8. Tim dropped his water bottle in the lake, but it did not **go below the surface of the water.**

    a. sink   b. soak   c. swim

9. Leah **accidentally made** the milk **flow from its container**, so she has to clean it up.

    a. sprinkled   b. squirted   c. spilled

10. Please tell me when the water **gets very hot, bubbles, and begins to turn to steam.**

    a. spills   b. sprinkles   c. boils

11. The water is **escaping through a hole** from the garden hose.

    a. leaking   b. pouring   c. melting

12. Danny's doctor suggested **using water to clean** his eye twice a day.

    a. sinking   b. bubbling   c. flushing

13. The milk **flowed in a thin stream** out of the baby's mouth.

    a. dribbled   b. soaked   c. boiled

14. The floor was **wet and difficult to walk on** after I mopped it.

    a. squirt   b. slick   c. sprinkle

15. When the water **began to form bubbles**, I added the vegetables to the pot.

    a. bubbled   b. soaked   c. melted

16. Before Teresa left for her date, she **put drops of** perfume behind her ears.

    a. rinsed   b. sprayed   c. poured

17. At the public pool, Peter learned to **move through the water using his arms and legs.**

    a. trickle   b. spill   c. swim

18. Angela **put** the greasy pots **in water and left them there.**

    a. drained   b. poured   c. soaked

19. He squeezed the bottle and mustard **came out of a narrow opening** onto his sandwich.

    a. squirted   b. melted   c. boiled

20. She **used a spoon to mix** the soup.

    a. dribbled   b. stirred   c. floated

21. The ice cubes were **difficult to pick up and hold**, so Helen kept dropping them.

    a. wet   b. bubble   c. slippery

22. The water in the pond **turned into ice.**

    a. froze   b. drained   c. leaked

23. After the interview, **a small amount of** sweat **flowed slowly** down his neck.

    a. melted   b. trickled   c. sprinkled

24. We **covered** the car **with water** so we could wash it.

    a. wet   b. sink   c. float

25. Paul asked the waiter to **lightly drop a little** oil and vinegar on his salad.

    a. flush   b. sprinkle   c. spill

B. Circle the word in each group that does not belong.

1. slick	sprinkle	slippery
2. flush	wet	soak
3. drip	freeze	melt
4. float	sink	soak
5. stir	boil	bubble
6. splash	drain	swim
7. dribble	trickle	squirt
8. spill	leak	pour
9. spray	drip	dive

Challenge Words

Check (✔) the words you already know.

☐ absorb   ☐ drench   ☐ ooze   ☐ submerge

☐ dissolve   ☐ evaporate   ☐ overflow   ☐ waterproof

296. Locations For / Near Water (Manmade)

Check (✔) the words you already know. Then, listen and repeat.

Tracks 1–5

☐ **aquarium**

TR 1

☐ **dock**

TR 2

Check Your Understanding

A. Choose the best word from the box to complete each sentence.

pool	aquarium	dock	dam	canal

1. The passengers waited for the ship to arrive at the _____.

2. I took my cousins to the _____ to see the penguins.

3. Everyone wanted to swim in the _____ and cool down.

4. The boat traveled through the _____ to get to the harbor.

5. The strong _____ held the water in the river back, and kept it from flowing.

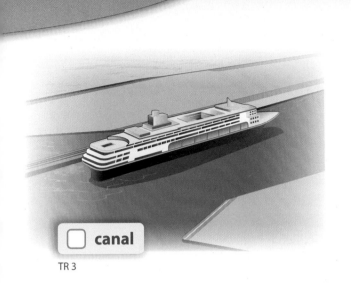

☐ **canal**

TR 3

☐ **dam**

TR 4

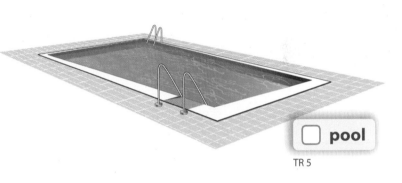

☐ **pool**

TR 5

Definitions

An **aquarium** is a building where fish and ocean animals live.

A **canal** is a long, narrow path filled with water that boats travel along.

A **dam** is a wall that is built across a river in order to stop water from flowing.

A **dock** is a structure at the edge of water where boats or ships stop for loading, unloading, or repairs.

A **pool**, or swimming pool, is a large hole filled with water that people can swim in.

B. Match each word to the correct description. One description will not be used.

1. _____ aquarium
2. _____ canal
3. _____ dam
4. _____ dock
5. _____ pool

a. a wall built across a river

b. a tower with a light that guides ships

c. a long, narrow path of water for boats to travel on

d. a place for people to go swimming in

e. a place where people can see fish and sea animals

f. a structure where boats stop for loading

Challenge Words

Check (✔) the words you already know.

☐ aqueduct   ☐ harbor   ☐ moat   ☐ reservoir   ☐ wharf

☐ channel   ☐ lighthouse   ☐ port   ☐ seaport

13

352. Equipment Used with Water / Liquid

Check (✔) the words you already know. Then, listen and repeat.

Tracks 1–3

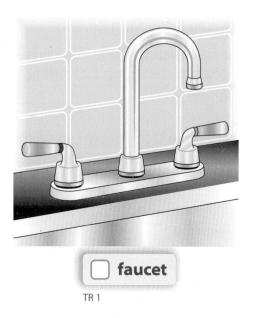

☐ **faucet**

TR 1

☐ **hose**

TR 2

Check Your Understanding

A. Complete the sentences.

1. Sprinklers and hoses are alike because _____
   _____
   _____.

2. Faucets and hoses are different because _____
   _____
   _____.

3. Faucets and hoses are alike because _____
   _____
   _____.

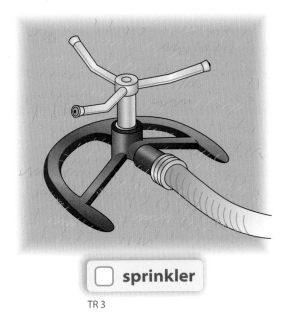

☐ **sprinkler**

TR 3

Definitions

A **faucet** is a device that controls the flow of a liquid from a pipe.

A **hose** is a long, flexible tube that water flows through. You can use a hose to spray water on plants or onto a fire.

A **sprinkler** is a device that sprays water over an area of grass or onto a fire.

B. Choose the sentence that correctly uses the underlined word.

1. a. The <u>sprinkler</u> in my kitchen sink was leaking.

   b. The <u>sprinkler</u> is watering the lawn.

2. a. Clara changed channels on the <u>faucet</u>.

   b. Charlie helped his dad fix their leaky bathroom <u>faucet</u>.

3. a. The <u>hose</u> was not long enough to reach the edge of the garden.

   b. We waited for the <u>hose</u> to stop at the traffic light.

Challenge Words

Check (✔) the words you already know.

☐ fountain   ☐ hydrant   ☐ nozzle   ☐ spout

☐ funnel   ☐ hydraulic   ☐ pump   ☐ valve

353. Moisture

Check (✔) the words you already know. Then, listen and repeat.

Tracks 1–2

☐ **cloud**

TR 1

☐ **fog**

TR 2

Definitions

A **cloud** is a white or gray mass in the sky that contains small drops of water.

Fog is a thick cloud that is close to the ground.

Check Your Understanding

A. Write **T** for **true statements** and **F** for **false statements**.

1. _____ Clouds are always white.

2. _____ Fog is close to the ground.

3. _____ Clouds have drops of water inside them.

4. _____ Fog is a thin cloud.

B. Choose the sentence that correctly uses the underlined word.

1. a. Irene drove carefully through the <u>fog</u>.

   b. She thought the <u>fog</u> would make it snow all day.

2. a. Mary's eyes hurt from the <u>clouds</u> in the sky.

   b. Paul saw the dark, heavy <u>clouds</u> and knew it was about to rain.

3. a. The weatherman said it would be very <u>foggy</u> and cold.

   b. It was very sunny and the sky was <u>foggy</u> all day.

4. a. John decided to go to the park to skateboard with his <u>cloudy</u> friends.

   b. Sharon was unhappy because it was <u>cloudy</u>, and she wanted to go to the beach.

Challenge Words

Check (✔) the words you already know.

☐ dew   ☐ smog

391. Water-Related Directions

Check (✔) the word if you already know it. Then, listen and repeat.

Track 1

☐ **afloat**

TR 1

Definition

Someone or something that is **afloat** is on the water.

Check Your Understanding

A. Check the items that you think would stay afloat in water.

☐ a beach ball   ☐ a raft   ☐ a rock   ☐ ice

☐ a boat   ☐ a chair   ☐ a quarter

B. Choose the sentence that correctly uses the underlined word.

1. a. Tim is <u>afloat</u> in the pool.

   b. She put her sandwich <u>afloat</u> the table.

2. a. The plane took <u>afloat</u> down the runway.

   b. The car could not stay <u>afloat</u> in the river.

3. a. The rock is <u>afloat</u> at the bottom of the stream.

   b. The rubber duck is <u>afloat</u> in the bathtub.

Challenge Words

Check (✔) the words you already know.

☐ ashore   ☐ downstream   ☐ inland   ☐ midstream   ☐ offshore

84. Sound Producing Devices

Check (✔) the words you already know. Then, listen and repeat.

Tracks 1–7

☐ **alarm**
TR 1

☐ **bell**
TR 3

☐ **siren**
TR 2

☐ **horn**
TR 4

Check Your Understanding

A. Underline the correct word to complete each sentence.

1. Henry used his (**horn / phone**) to call the doctor's office.

2. When the workers heard the fire (**alarm / phone**), they left the building quickly.

3. We heard several (**doorbells / sirens**), and then four police cars drove by.

4. The cat wears a (**telephone / bell**) around its neck. Every time he moves it makes a nice ringing sound.

5. The (**telephone / siren**) rang three times before Susana answered it.

6. I rang the (**doorbell / horn**) twice, but nobody came to open the door.

7. My grandfather honked the car (**horn / alarm**) to warn the driver of the car next to us.

B. Choose the sentence that correctly uses the underlined word.

1. a. When the <u>doorbell</u> rang, Mary went to open the door.

   b. She decided to turn on the <u>doorbell</u> and listen to it.

2. a. We used a <u>siren</u> to call our friends and family to invite them to a party.

   b. The police <u>siren</u> warned the drivers to move out of the way.

phone
telephone

TR 5 and TR 6

doorbell

TR 7

Definitions

An **alarm** is a device that warns people of danger, for example, by making a noise.

A **bell** is a hollow metal object that makes a sound when hit.

A **doorbell** is a bell next to a door that you can ring to tell the people inside that you are there.

A **horn** is an object in a car or another vehicle that makes a loud noise, and that is used to warn others of danger.

A **phone** or **telephone** is an electronic device that you use to talk to someone in another place.

A **siren** is a loud, high-pitched alarm on a fire truck, ambulance, or police car that is used to warn people.

3. a. The <u>horn</u> was used to wash the car.

b. The driver honked his <u>horn</u> to get the traffic moving.

4. a. The <u>bell</u> rang to announce that the next class was starting.

b. The children kicked the <u>bell</u> to try to make a goal.

5. a. Since the battery was low, he needed to charge his <u>phone</u>.

b. The <u>phone</u> warned that the cars needed to get out of the way.

6. a. To make sure that he got up on time, Peter set the <u>alarm</u> on his clock.

b. Erik honked his <u>alarm</u> to warn the cars that he was turning left.

7. a. Susan wanted to watch the <u>telephone</u> with her brothers after school.

b. If you are late, it is important to call on the <u>telephone</u> to let someone know.

Challenge Words

Check (✔) the words you already know.

chime

earphone

firebox

gong

loudspeaker

sonar

103. Noises (General)

Check (✔) the words you already know. Then, listen and repeat.

Tracks 1–11

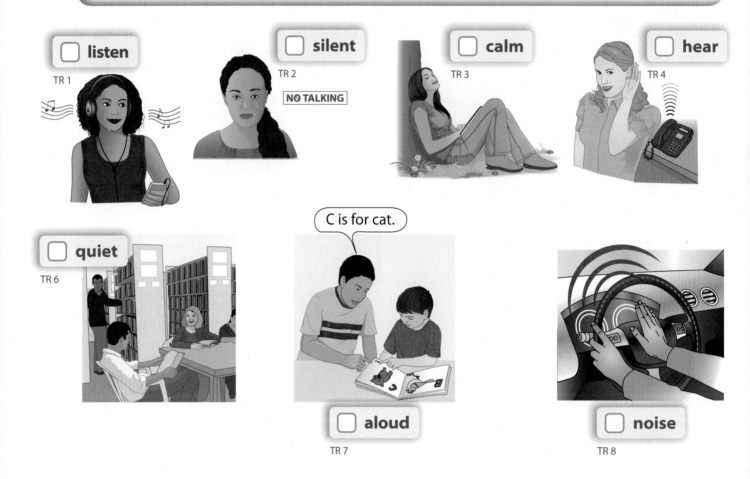

☐ listen
TR 1

☐ silent
TR 2
NO TALKING

☐ calm
TR 3

☐ hear
TR 4

☐ quiet
TR 6

C is for cat.

☐ aloud
TR 7

☐ noise
TR 8

Check Your Understanding

A. Underline the correct word to complete each sentence.

1. People respectfully stood in (**silence / aloud**) as the president entered the room.

2. Wendy heard a loud (**noise / listen**) like a big bang.

3. Paul shouted in the canyon to hear his voice (**echo / calm**).

4. The children were reminded to be (**silent / loud**) during the assembly.

5. When it was Tony's turn to read (**echo / aloud**), he was nervous.

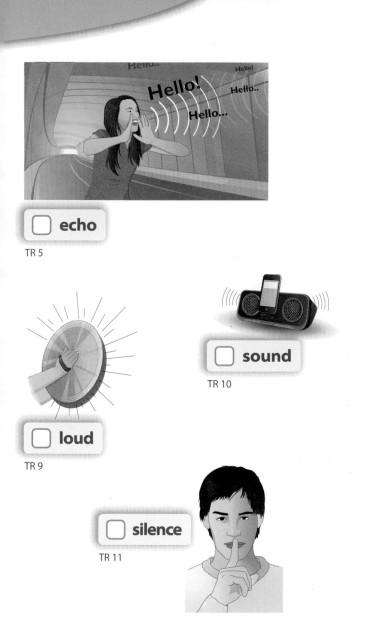

TR 5

□ echo

□ loud

TR 9

□ sound

TR 10

□ silence

TR 11

Definitions

When you speak, read, or laugh **aloud**, other people can hear you.

A **calm** person is not worried, angry, or excited.

An **echo** is a sound that you hear again because it bounces off a hard surface.

To **hear** something, like a sound, means to receive sound with the ears.

To **listen** to something or someone means to give your attention to a sound or to what someone is saying.

When a noise is **loud**, the level of sound is very high.

Noise is a sound, especially a loud or an unpleasant one.

Someone or something that is **quiet** makes only a small amount of noise or is silent.

When there is **silence**, there is no noise at all.

When you are **silent**, you are not making any noise.

A **sound** is something that you can hear.

6. Jenny could (**hear** / **sound**) someone knocking on her door.

7. The baby is sleeping, so we must be (**noise** / **quiet**).

8. David remained (**calm** / **echo**) during the meeting with his boss.

9. What kind of (**listen** / **sound**) does a rooster make?

10. It is a good idea to stop, look, and (**noise** / **listen**) before crossing a street.

11. Charlie is a (**silent** / **loud**) person who likes to tell stories and jokes.

B. Match each word to the correct description. One description will not be used.

1. _____ calm
2. _____ aloud
3. _____ loud
4. _____ noise
5. _____ silent
6. _____ echo
7. _____ listen
8. _____ hear
9. _____ sound
10. _____ silence
11. _____ quiet

a. level of sound is very high

b. no noise at all

c. something you can hear

d. not worried, angry, or excited

e. to speak or laugh so others can hear

f. a sound that repeats

g. to receive a sound through your ears

h. to give your attention to a sound or to what someone is saying

i. to listen secretly to a private conversation

j. an unpleasant sound

k. someone who makes little or no noise

l. no one speaking

Challenge Words

Check (✔) the words you already know.

☐ audio   ☐ commotion   ☐ harsh   ☐ serene

☐ clatter   ☐ eavesdrop   ☐ hush   ☐ tranquil

156. Noises that People Make

Check (✔) the words you already know. Then, listen and repeat.

Tracks 1–18

☐ laughter
TR 2

☐ cough
TR 4

☐ cheer
TR 1

☐ laugh
TR 3

☐ snore
TR 5

☐ yell
TR 6

☐ shout
TR 7

☐ holler
TR 8

☐ giggle
TR 9

☐ roar
TR 11

☐ sing
TR 10

☐ applause
TR 12

23

☐ chuckle
TR 13

☐ whisper
TR 14

☐ yawn
TR 15

☐ whistle
TR 16

☐ cry
TR 17

☐ scream
TR 18

Definitions

Applause is the noise that a group of people make when they all clap their hands together to show that they like something.

To **cheer** means to shout loudly to show that you are pleased or to encourage someone.

To **chuckle** means to laugh quietly.

To **cough** means to suddenly force air out of your throat with a noise.

When you **cry**, tears come from your eyes and you make a sound with your mouth in pain or fear.

To **giggle** means to laugh in a silly way like a child.

To **holler** means to shout loudly.

To **laugh** means to make a sound while smiling to show that you think something is funny.

Laughter is the sound of people laughing.

If a person **roars**, they make a loud, scary sound.

To **scream** means to make a loud, high cry because you are hurt or frightened.

To **shout** means to say something very loudly.

To **sing** means to make music with your voice.

When someone **snores**, that person makes noise each time they breathe while they are asleep.

To **whisper** is to say something very quietly.

To **whistle** is to make musical sounds by blowing your breath out between your lips.

To **yawn** means to open your mouth very wide and breathe in more air than usual because you are tired.

To **yell** means to shout loudly.

24

Check Your Understanding

A. Match each word to the correct description. One description will be used twice, and one description will not be used at all.

1. _____ cheer
2. _____ laugh
3. _____ shout
4. _____ whisper
5. _____ applause
6. _____ cough
7. _____ holler
8. _____ scream
9. _____ whistle
10. _____ yawn
11. _____ snore
12. _____ laughter
13. _____ giggle
14. _____ chuckle
15. _____ yell
16. _____ sing
17. _____ roar
18. _____ cry

a. to have tears come from your eyes
b. to make music with your voice
c. to shout loudly
d. when a person makes a loud, scary noise
e. to open your mouth very wide and breathe in more air than usual
f. to laugh in a silly way
g. the sound of people laughing
h. to make noise while sleeping
i. to make sounds by blowing your breath out between your teeth
j. to shout loudly to show that you are pleased
k. the noise made when a group of people clap their hands together
l. to say something very quietly
m. to suddenly force air out of your throat
n. to say something very loudly
o. to make a sound while smiling
p. to speak quietly and not clearly
q. to laugh quietly
r. to make a loud, high cry when afraid

B. Circle the correct word to complete each sentence.

1. The fans _____ when their favorite team entered the stadium.
   a. cheered   b. snored   c. coughed

2. The man _____ as he watched a funny show on TV.
   a. shouted   b. hollered   c. chuckled

3. Everyone started to _____ when they heard the sad news.
   a. applause   b. whistle   c. cry

4. The audience was so pleased with the performance that the _____ lasted for several minutes.
   a. laughter   b. applause   c. yawn

5. The engine noise was so loud that the workers had to _____ to hear one another.
   a. sing   b. yell   c. chuckle

6. Matthew and Phillip didn't want anyone to hear their conversation, so they had to _____ .

   a. whisper   b. yawn   c. laugh

7. The choir began to _____ a beautiful song.

   a. sing   b. roar   c. cry

8. The classroom was so loud that the teacher had to _____ to get his students' attention.

   a. giggle   b. whisper   c. shout

9. I knew my parents were sleepy because they _____ several times.

   a. screamed   b. yawned   c. cheered

10. Jack began to _____ as he breathed in the smoke from the grill.

    a. cough   b. whistle   c. snore

11. The children started to _____ as they watched the silly cartoon.

    a. holler   b. sing   c. giggle

12. Kyle _____ at his friends to wait for him, but they were too far away to hear.

    a. laughed   b. hollered   c. yawned

13. The frightened mother _____ when she saw her baby was hurt.

    a. screamed   b. cheered   c. giggled

14. The hiker _____ a happy song as he walked along the trail.

    a. whistled   b. giggled   c. cried

15. My father always _____ while he sleeps.

    a. roars   b. yawns   c. snores

16. We heard _____ coming from the garden, so we knew the children were playing happily.

    a. crying   b. laughter   c. coughing

17. Steve hid behind the couch and _____ to scare his sister when she came into the room.

    a. roared   b. cheered   c. chuckled

18. The audience _____ at the performer's funny jokes.

    a. yelled   b. snored   c. laughed

Challenge Words

Check (✔) the words you already know.

☐ applaud   ☐ hiccup   ☐ mutter   ☐ shriek   ☐ weep

☐ burp   ☐ mumble   ☐ ovation   ☐ squeal   ☐ whine

165. Noises That Objects Make

Check (✔) the words you already know. Then, listen and repeat.

Tracks 1–13

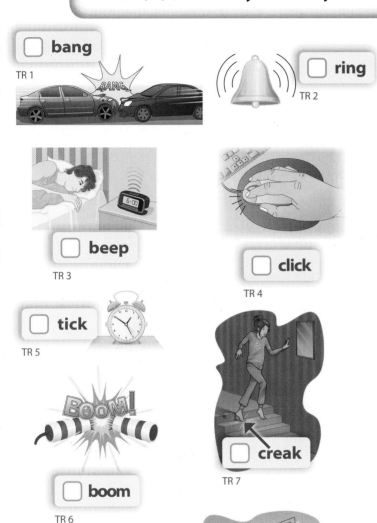

☐ **bang**
TR 1

☐ **ring**
TR 2

☐ **beep**
TR 3

☐ **click**
TR 4

☐ **tick**
TR 5

☐ **creak**
TR 7

☐ **boom**
TR 6

Definitions

A **bang** is a sudden, loud noise.

A **beep** is a short, high sound made by an electronic device.

A **boom** is a deep, loud noise.

A **click** is a short, sharp sound.

A **creak** is a short, high sound something makes when you move or step on it.

A **plop** is the soft sound of something dropping into water.

A **rattle** is a series of repeated noises made when one hard object hits against another.

A **ring** is a sound like the noise of a bell.

A **slam** is a very loud noise.

A **squeak** is a short, high sound. Some animals, such as mice, make a **squeak**.

A **tick** is the series of short sounds a clock makes as it works.

A **toot** is a short sound made by a car horn.

A **zoom** is a sound made by something moving very quickly.

☐ **plop**
TR 8

☐ **slam**
TR 9

☐ **zoom**
TR 10

☐ **rattle**
TR 11

☐ **toot**
TR 12

☐ **squeak**
TR 13

Check Your Understanding

A. Choose the sentence that correctly uses the underlined word.

1. a. I was so angry that I shut the door with a <u>slam</u>.

   b. The <u>slam</u> went through the window.

2. a. I pressed the car horn and heard a <u>rattle</u>.

   b. The music was so loud that I could hear the <u>rattle</u> of the plates on the shelf.

3. a. The rubber duck toy landed in the bath with a <u>plop</u>.

   b. When Marcus played football, he liked to throw and <u>plop</u> the ball.

4. a. I heard a <u>creak</u> when the old, heavy door opened.

   b. Derek likes watching the cars <u>creak</u> around the racetrack.

5. a. After she heard the <u>click</u>, Gail knew that the seat belt was secure.

   b. We all heard the <u>click</u> as Jane's keys fell into the lake.

6. a. The door opened and Fred heard the <u>tick</u> of someone walking up the stairs.

   b. The soft <u>tick</u> of the clock kept Marissa awake all night.

7. a. Every day at noon, we can hear the <u>ring</u> of the bells in the town square.

   b. Andrea tripped and fell to the ground with a loud <u>ring</u>.

8. a. There was a <u>squeak</u> on each person's dinner plate.

   b. The mouse made a few <u>squeaks</u> as Justin picked him up.

9. a. The <u>boom</u> from the explosion was heard throughout the neighborhood.

   b. Marcus knew his suitcase was shut when he heard it <u>boom</u>.

10. a. The <u>toot</u> from the approaching car made everyone stop and look.

    b. The seashells made a <u>toot</u> as Carla threw them in the bucket.

11. a. My father woke up when he heard the <u>zoom</u> of the telephone.

    b. The <u>zoom</u> of the motorcycles startled the people on the sidewalk.

12. a. When the car accidentally crashed into the mailbox, I heard a loud <u>bang</u>.

    b. Gary heard his watch <u>bang</u> and knew he had to hurry.

13. a. The swing made a <u>beep</u> as it swung back and forth.

    b. I heard a <u>beep</u> from the oven and I knew the food was ready.

B. Underline the correct word to complete each sentence.

1. We heard a few (**plops** / **creaks**) as the cook dropped some carrots into the pot of soup.

2. They heard a loud (**creak** / **zoom**) as the police car raced down the street.

3. John woke up when he heard the (**beep** / **boom**) of his alarm.

4. The little boy had to be reminded not to close the door with a (**ring** / **slam**).

5. The loud (**tick** / **toot**) of the school clock made the boy nervous as he took the exam.

6. The pet hamster gave a (**squeak** / **tick**) as Michael opened the cage.

7. The little girl covered her ears when she heard the (**zoom** / **boom**) of the thunder.

8. The old wooden door made a long (**beep** / **creak**) as I pushed it open.

9. The (**ring** / **squeak**) of the alarm bell was heard throughout the building.

10. Today was so windy that I could hear the (**plop** / **rattle**) of the windows.

11. The song began suddenly with the loud (**ring** / **bang**) of the drum.

12. Henry knew the door was closed when he heard the (**click** / **boom**) of the lock.

13. The (**slam** / **toot**) of a car horn outside woke Rachel up from her nap.

Challenge Words

Check (✔) the words you already know.

☐ clang   ☐ crunch   ☐ jingle   ☐ swish
☐ clink   ☐ gurgle   ☐ rustle   ☐ thump

175. Noises that Animals Make

Check (✔) the words you already know. Then, listen and repeat.

Tracks 1–11

☐ meow

TR 1

☐ growl

TR 2

☐ moo

TR 3

☐ bark

TR 7

☐ purr

TR 8

☐ baa

TR 9

Check Your Understanding

A. Choose the best word from the word bank to complete each sentence. One word will not be used.

meows	croak	growls	moos
peep	purr	gobbles	clucks
barks	baas	buzzed	quack

1. My dog's _____ is loud and excited.

2. Carol could hear her cat's _____ as she patted its back.

3. When we got near the barn, we heard the chicken's soft _____ .

4. The cowboys love to listen to the _____ of the cows.

5. The bees' _____ could be heard as they went from flower to flower.

6. I could hear the duck's _____ as it landed near the pond.

7. After the bird egg hatched, the kids heard the baby bird's _____ .

cluck
TR 4

gobble
TR 5

peep
TR 6

buzz
TR 10

quack
TR 11

Definitions

Baa is the sound that a sheep makes.

A **bark** is a short, loud noise that a dog makes.

A **buzz** is a long, continuous sound, like the noise a bee makes when it flies.

A **cluck** is the sound that a chicken makes.

A **gobble** is the sound that a turkey makes.

A **growl** is a low noise made in an animal's throat because it is angry.

Meow is the sound that a cat makes.

A **moo** is the long, low sound that a cow makes.

A **peep** is a short, high sound that a young bird makes.

A **purr** is the low sound that a cat makes in its throat when it is happy.

A **quack** is the sound that a duck makes.

8. The turkeys' _____ became louder when they saw the farmer coming with their food.

9. The sheep's _____ made it easy to find on the hillside.

10. The loud _____ from her cat let Judy know that he was ready to come inside the house.

11. The low, angry _____ from the two dogs scared the robber away.

B. Match each word to the correct description. One description will not be used.

1. _____ quack   a. sound that a horse makes

2. _____ peep   b. sound that a dog makes

3. _____ gobble   c. sound that a bee makes

4. _____ baa   d. sound that a cat makes

5. _____ meow   e. sound that a cow makes

6. _____ bark   f. sound that a sheep makes

7. _____ buzz   g. sound that a chicken makes

8. _____ moo   h. sound that a turkey makes

9. _____ cluck   i. a low noise in the throat, like an angry dog or other animal makes

10. _____ growl   j. sound that a little bird makes

11. _____ purr   k. a low noise in the throat, like a happy cat makes

     l. sound that a duck makes

Challenge Words

Check (✔) the words you already know.

☐ cackle   ☐ croak   ☐ honk   ☐ whinny

☐ chirp   ☐ grunt   ☐ howl   ☐ yowl

48. Types of Meals

Check (✔) the words you already know. Then, listen and repeat.

Tracks 1–8

☐ **meal**

TR 1

☐ **picnic**

TR 2

☐ **treat**

TR 3

☐ **dessert**

TR 4

Definitions

Breakfast is the first meal of the day.

Dessert is something sweet that you eat at the end of a meal.

Dinner is the main meal of the day, usually served in the evening.

Lunch is the meal that you have in the middle of the day.

A **meal** is an occasion when people sit down and eat.

A **picnic** is a meal prepared ahead of time and eaten outdoors, usually in a park or a forest, or at the beach.

Supper is a meal that people eat in the evening. *Supper* means the same as *dinner*.

A **treat** is something that tastes good and that is not eaten often.

☐ **breakfast**

TR 5

☐ **lunch**

TR 6

☐ **dinner**
☐ **supper**

TR 7 and TR 8

Check Your Understanding

A. Match each word to the correct description. One description will not be used.

1. _____ breakfast
2. _____ lunch
3. _____ meal
4. _____ picnic
5. _____ dessert
6. _____ dinner
7. _____ treat
8. _____ supper

a. a meal eaten at an outdoor location, such as a park

b. the first meal of the day

c. a meal that is arranged on a long table at a party and the guests serve themselves

d. the main meal of the day, usually served in the evening

e. an evening meal similar to dinner

f. the meal you have in the middle of the day

g. something special to eat

h. something sweet that you eat after a meal

i. an occasion when people sit and eat

B. Underline the correct word to complete each sentence.

1. The children were each given a cookie as a (**lunch / treat**).

2. After dinner, Greg ordered an ice cream for (**picnic / dessert**).

3. That night, the family went to a Chinese restaurant for (**dinner / breakfast**).

4. The friends ate (**lunch / meal**) together at noon.

5. Harry and his dad met in the evening for (**breakfast / supper**).

6. The (**picnic / treat**) at the park was canceled because of the rain.

7. The cafeteria only serves two (**desserts / meals**) a day: breakfast and lunch.

8. Carla woke up at seven in the morning and ate (**breakfast / supper**).

Challenge Words

Check (✔) the words you already know.

☐ banquet   ☐ buffet   ☐ chow   ☐ feast   ☐ refreshment

51. Eating and Drinking

Check (✔) the words you already know. Then, listen and repeat.

 Tracks 1–7

☐ **sip**
TR 1

Definitions

To **bite** into food means to use your teeth to cut into it or through it.

To **chew** something means to break it up with your teeth.

To **drink** a liquid means to take it into your mouth and swallow it.

To **eat** food means to put it into your mouth and swallow it.

To **feed** someone means to give that person food.

To **sip** a drink means to drink it slowly, taking a small amount at a time.

To **swallow** food or drink means to make it go from your mouth into your throat and then into your stomach.

☐ **bite**
TR 2

☐ **drink**
TR 3

☐ **swallow**
TR 4

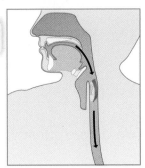

☐ **chew**
TR 5

☐ **eat**
TR 6

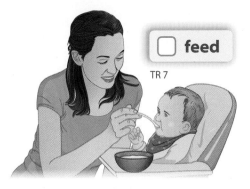

☐ **feed**
TR 7

Check Your Understanding

A. Match each word to the correct description. One description will not be used.

1. _____ bite
2. _____ eat
3. _____ sip
4. _____ chew
5. _____ drink
6. _____ feed
7. _____ swallow

a. to take a liquid into your mouth and swallow it

b. to give a person food

c. to make food go from your mouth into your throat and then into your stomach

d. to use your teeth to cut into or through food

e. to put food in your mouth and swallow it

f. to take a liquid in your mouth, move it around in your throat, and spit it out

g. to break food up with your teeth

h. to drink slowly, taking a small amount at a time

B. Underline the correct word to complete each sentence.

1. George lifted the cup of hot tea, put it to his lips, and began to (**sip / eat**).

2. The steak was hard for Mandy to (**drink / chew**).

3. We bought enough food to (**sip / feed**) the whole family for a week.

4. I like to (**drink / chew**) coffee and juice in the morning.

5. As soon as Emily (**swallowed / fed**) the medicine, she felt it begin to work.

6. The man took a (**sip / bite**) of the hamburger.

7. My uncle is a vegetarian, so he doesn't (**eat / drink**) meat.

Challenge Words

Check (✔) the words you already know.

☐ consume ☐ dine ☐ gnaw ☐ guzzle ☐ nibble

☐ devour ☐ gargle ☐ gorge ☐ munch

74. Ingredients Used to Make Food

Check (✔) the words you already know. Then, listen and repeat.

Tracks 1–11

☐ **dough**
TR 1

☐ **flour**
TR 2

☐ **gravy**
TR 3

☐ **pepper**
TR 4

☐ **mix**
TR 5

☐ **salt**
TR 6

☐ **ketchup**
TR 7

☐ **mayonnaise**
TR 8

☐ **mustard**
TR 9

☐ **sugar**
TR 10

☐ **sauce**
TR 11

Definitions

Dough is a mixture of flour, water, and other things that can be cooked to make bread and cakes.

Flour is a fine powder that is used for making bread, cakes, and pastry.

Gravy is a sauce made from the juices and fats from cooked meat.

Ketchup is a thick, red sauce made from tomatoes.

Mayonnaise is a cold, thick, white sauce made from eggs and oil.

A **mix** is a dry mixture of ingredients that you use in order to make something. When you want to use it, you add liquid.

Mustard is a spicy yellow or brown sauce that you eat with meat.

Pepper is a spice with a hot taste that you put on food.

Salt is a white substance that you use to improve the flavor of food.

A **sauce** is a thick liquid that is poured over food.

Sugar is a sweet substance that is used for making food and drinks taste sweet.

Check Your Understanding

A. Match each word to the correct description. One description will not be used.

1. _____ pepper
2. _____ mayonnaise
3. _____ sugar
4. _____ sauce
5. _____ dough
6. _____ mustard
7. _____ mix
8. _____ gravy
9. _____ ketchup
10. _____ flour
11. _____ salt

a. cold, thick, white sauce made from eggs and oil

b. spicy yellow or brown sauce eaten with meat

c. thick liquid that is poured over food

d. white substance that you use to make food taste better

e. thick, red sauce made from tomatoes

f. mixture of flour and water that can be cooked to make bread and cakes

g. fine powder that is used for making pastries

h. dry mixture of ingredients that comes in a package

i. substance that is used for making food and drinks taste sweet

j. sour, sharp-tasting liquid that is used in cooking

k. spice with a hot taste

l. sauce made from the juices that come from meat when it cooks

B. Write **T** for **true statements** and **F** for **false statements**.

1. _____ Gravy is a spice with a very hot taste.
2. _____ Mustard is usually eaten with meat.
3. _____ If you want your coffee to taste sweet, you should add some sugar.
4. _____ Sometimes, when people want to make their food taste hot, they add pepper.
5. _____ Flour and water are the main ingredients of mayonnaise.
6. _____ Dough can be cooked to make bread.
7. _____ Salt is a yellow substance that is used to make food taste good.
8. _____ Ketchup is a thick, red sauce made from meat juices.
9. _____ Bread, cakes, and pastries are made from flour.
10. _____ Sauce is usually eaten on its own.
11. _____ A mix usually has a combination of wet and dry ingredients.

Challenge Words

Check (✔) the words you already know.

- [ ] batter
- [ ] cinnamon
- [ ] garlic
- [ ] graham
- [ ] shortening
- [ ] spice
- [ ] starch
- [ ] vinegar
- [ ] yeast

86. Dairy Products

Check (✔) the words you already know. Then, listen and repeat.

Tracks 1–6

☐ **egg**

TR 1

☐ **yolk**

TR 2

Definitions

Butter is a soft, yellow food made from cream. You spread it on bread or use it in cooking.

Cheese is a solid food made from milk.

Cream is a thick liquid that is made from the fat of milk.

An **egg** is something that people eat and that comes from a bird-like animal, such as a hen.

Margarine is a yellow substance that is made from vegetable oil and is a substitute for butter.

The **yolk** is the yellow part of an egg.

☐ **cheese**

TR 3

☐ **butter**

TR 4

☐ **margarine**

TR 5

☐ **cream**

TR 6

Check Your Understanding

A. Write **T** for **true statements** and **F** for **false statements**.

1. _____ A yolk comes from the inside of an egg.

2. _____ Cheese is made from milk.

3. _____ Eggs are a popular drink in many countries.

4. _____ Margarine can be used in place of butter.

5. _____ Butter and margarine are both made from cream.

6. _____ Cream comes from a bird-like animal, such as a hen.

B. Circle the correct word to complete each sentence.

1. Frank likes to spread _____ on his bread.

   a. cream   b. butter   c. yolk

2. Suzy carefully cracked open the egg, and the _____ fell out into a small bowl.

   a. milk   b. margarine   c. yolk

3. Butter tastes best when it is made from fresh _____ .

   a. cream   b. cheese   c. egg

4. What kind of oil is used to make _____ ?

   a. cheese   b. egg   c. margarine

5. Daniela ordered fried _____ for breakfast.

   a. eggs   b. butter   c. margarine

6. Yesterday I ate a ham and _____ sandwich.

   a. yolk   b. cream   c. cheese

Challenge Words

Check (✔) the word if you already know it.

☐ curd

124. Foods that Are Prepared

Check (✔) the words you already know. Then, listen and repeat.

 Tracks 1–28

☐ **bread**
TR 1

☐ **hamburger**
TR 3

☐ **hotdog**
TR 5

☐ **cracker**
TR 7

☐ **muffin**
TR 9

☐ **chips**
TR 11

☐ **biscuit**
TR 13

☐ **jelly**
TR 2

☐ **coleslaw**
TR 4

☐ **crust**
TR 6

☐ **loaf**
TR 8

☐ **bun**
TR 10

☐ **macaroni**
TR 12

☐ **cereal**
TR 14

Definitions

A **biscuit** is a small, round, airy roll of bread.

Bread is a food made mostly from flour and water.

A **bun** is bread in a small, round shape.

Cereal is a food made from grain that you add milk to and eat for breakfast.

Chips or potato chips are very thin slices of fried potato.

Coleslaw is a salad made from pieces of raw carrot and cabbage, mixed with a mayonnaise sauce.

A **cracker** is a thin, hard piece of baked bread that can be eaten with cheese.

The **crust** on a loaf of bread is the hard outer part.

A **hamburger** is made from small pieces of chopped meat that have been shaped into a flat circle. A hamburger is fried or grilled and is often served on a round piece of bread (called a roll or a bun).

A **hotdog** is a small, cooked sausage that is usually served in a bun.

Jelly is a sweet food made by cooking fruit with a large amount of sugar. Jelly is usually spread on bread.

A **loaf**, such as a loaf of bread, is bread that has been baked and formed into one shape.

Macaroni is a type of pasta made in the shape of short, hollow tubes.

A **muffin** is a small, round, sweet cake that often has fruit inside of it. People usually eat muffins for breakfast.

noodle
TR 15

salad
TR 16

omelet
TR 17

oatmeal
TR 18

taco
TR 19

spaghetti
TR 20

tortilla
TR 21

waffle
TR 22

pretzel
TR 23

pancake
TR 24

snack
TR 25

toast
TR 26

pizza
TR 27

sandwich
TR 28

Definitions

A **noodle** is a long, narrow or wide, flat strip of pasta made from a mixture of flour, egg, and water. Noodles are often used in Chinese and Italian cooking.

Oatmeal is a hot, thick food often eaten for breakfast. It is made from oats cooked in water or milk.

An **omelet** is a fried dish made of eggs often served folded over a filling, such as cheese.

A **pancake** is a thin, flat, round cooked food made from milk, flour, and eggs. People often eat pancakes for breakfast with butter and syrup.

A **pizza** is a flat, round piece of bread that is covered with tomatoes, cheese, and sometimes other foods, and then baked in an oven.

A **pretzel** is a crisp or chewy bread-like food, usually shaped like a knot and sprinkled with salt on the outside.

A **salad** is a mixture of foods, especially vegetables, that is usually served cold.

A **sandwich** is two slices of bread with another food, such as cheese, meat, or vegetables, between them.

A **snack** is a small amount of food that is quick to prepare and usually eaten between meals.

Spaghetti is a type of pasta that looks like long pieces of string.

A **taco** is a thin, flat pancake made of flour or cornmeal, filled with meat and vegetables.

Toast is a slice of bread that has been heated until it is brown.

A **tortilla** is a Mexican bread of corn meal made in a thin layer and cooked on a grill.

A **waffle** is a flat, sweet cake with a pattern of squares on it that is usually eaten warm with syrup for breakfast.

Check Your Understanding

A. Underline the correct word to complete each sentence.

1. The first step of making (**pancakes / hamburgers**) is to shape the meat into flat circles.

2. Alexander cut the (**bun / jelly**) in half and put butter on it.

3. In order to make (**chips / hotdogs**), the potatoes must be sliced very thinly before they are fried.

4. Chris spread some grape (**macaroni / jelly**) on his toast.

5. I prefer to eat (**salad / pancakes**) with butter and syrup.

6. Between lunch and dinner, Sara ate an apple for a (**snack / crust**).

7. My father usually eats warm (**toast / coleslaw**) for breakfast.

8. There was a delicious smell of (**pizza / salad**) baking in the oven.

9. Nick put mustard and ketchup on his (**waffle / hotdog**).

10. The (**biscuits / jellies**) were so dry that they made Helena very thirsty.

11. Regina bought a (**waffle / loaf**) of bread at the bakery.

12. Carl ate a small, salty (**muffin / pretzel**).

13. For breakfast, everyone was served a warm bowl of (**oatmeal / crust**).

14. The boy spooned up some (**muffins / noodles**) from his bowl of soup.

15. The cook stirred some mayonnaise into the bowl, and then the (**coleslaw / cereal**) was done.

16. Justine poured some tomato sauce over her (**cereal / macaroni**).

17. Lawrence started making the (**omelet / sandwich**) by beating three eggs in a small bowl.

18. For breakfast, we had a choice between blueberry or banana (**muffins / spaghetti**).

19. Corn is often used to make a thin, flat bread called a (**bun / tortilla**).

20. A (**pancake / waffle**) has a pattern of squares on it.

21. Veronica ordered a plate of (**tacos / pretzels**) at the Mexican restaurant.

22. Janie thinks that (**spaghetti / macaroni**) is fun to eat because it is so long and thin.

23. (**Oatmeal / Bread**) is a food made mostly from flour and water.

24. I like to eat a cold breakfast: (**cereal / hamburger**) with milk.

25. Anne cut the hard (**loaf / crust**) off her bread before she ate it.

26. The cold, crisp (**omelet / salad**) had lettuce and cucumbers in it.

27. Carl put mustard on his ham and cheese (**sandwich / chip**) and cut it in half.

28. For a snack, Ed put a piece of cheese on top of a (**pizza / cracker**).

B. Choose the sentence that correctly uses the underlined word.

1. a. He ordered more <u>toast</u> to go with his breakfast.

   b. The <u>toast</u> is where water meets land.

2. a. Terri used the <u>bread</u> to paint the walls of her house.

   b. Lisa used two slices of <u>bread</u> to make a ham and cheese sandwich.

3. a. Tom ordered a <u>hotdog</u> with mustard.

   b. The <u>hotdog</u> dropped money and ran away.

4. a. Harry added ice cubes to his <u>pancake</u> and drank it.

   b. My <u>pancake</u> has butter and syrup on it.

5. a. For lunch, we ate a ham and cheese <u>sandwich</u>.

   b. A <u>sandwich</u> is a type of large, hairy dog.

6. a. He put the small balls of <u>salad</u> in the fire, and they exploded.

   b. She put a creamy dressing on her green <u>salad</u>.

7. a. I like grape <u>jelly</u> on my toast.

   b. The <u>jelly</u> soared high in the sky, before it fell to the ground.

8. a. The cook was careful when he took the cheese <u>pizza</u> out of the oven.

   b. The chef stirred the <u>pizza</u> as it boiled in the cooking pot.

9. a. The man took the <u>snack</u> out of his toolbox and used it to fix the door.

   b. At school, the students eat a <u>snack</u> before lunchtime.

10. a. Charlie asked for another <u>biscuit</u> to eat with his fried chicken.

    b. I used a <u>biscuit</u> to clean my bathroom floor.

11. a. The hungry <u>omelet</u> ate the rooster and the hen.

    b. My bacon and cheese <u>omelet</u> is delicious!

12. a. Mary made the <u>coleslaw</u> with cabbage, carrots, and mayonnaise.

    b. The <u>coleslaw</u> wandered through the wet forest looking for the king.

13. a. Will you heat up the <u>macaroni</u> and cheese for dinner?

    b. Fred paid the <u>macaroni</u> and left the store.

14. a. The <u>loaf</u> of bread is enough to make six sandwiches.

    b. At the football game, Bob threw the <u>loaf</u> to his teammate.

15. a. As he ate the spaghetti, a long <u>noodle</u> stuck on his chin.

    b. The <u>noodle</u> played the drums at the parade.

16. a. He used the <u>pretzel</u> to open the large, heavy door.

    b. David gave his son a small, crispy <u>pretzel</u>.

17. a. Eric waited for the <u>oatmeal</u> to cool a bit before he ate it.

    b. They replaced the flat tire with <u>oatmeal</u> and drove off.

18. a. Kate rested her feet on the <u>muffin</u> and began knitting.

    b. His favorite type of <u>muffin</u> is banana.

19. a. A <u>waffle</u> and the hammer swam across the pond.

    b. I like to top my <u>waffles</u> with butter, syrup, and fresh fruit.

20. a. Brad used the <u>spaghetti</u> to climb to the top of the mountain.

    b. I think the <u>spaghetti</u> needs more tomato sauce and meatballs.

21. a. My favorite <u>taco</u> is made with pork, lettuce, cheese, and salsa.

    b. The <u>taco</u> opened its wings and tweeted before it took off.

22. a. We upset the <u>tortilla</u> when we didn't invite it to the carnival.

    b. I think a <u>tortilla</u> tastes better after it is warmed up.

23. a. The <u>hamburgers</u> were cooked outside on the grill.

    b. It was the <u>hamburger</u> that robbed the bank.

24. a. Kelly bought a dozen hamburger <u>buns</u> for the party.

    b. The <u>buns</u> hopped through the grassy field.

25. a. Some children do not like the <u>crust</u> of bread because it can be hard to chew.

    b. He added <u>crust</u> to the engine before he turned the key.

26. a. The <u>cereal</u> rode the brown bike faster than the girl.

    b. The <u>cereal</u> needed more milk and sugar.

27. a. The <u>cracker</u> was framed and shown at the fine art museum.

    b. James put thin slices of cheese on the <u>crackers</u>.

28. a. <u>Chips</u> are an excellent drink during hot days.

    b. Sarah ate a small bag of <u>chips</u> with her sandwich.

Challenge Words

Check (✔) the words you already know.

☐ flapjack ☐ lasagna ☐ porridge

☐ gruel ☐ mush ☐ watercress

136. Meats

Check (✔) the words you already know. Then, listen and repeat.

Tracks 1–8

☐ **steak**
TR 1

☐ **bologna**
TR 2

☐ **sausage**
TR 3

☐ **bacon**
TR 4

Check Your Understanding

A. Choose the sentence that correctly uses the underlined word.

1. a. The strips of cooked <u>bacon</u> added a salty flavor to the hamburger.

   b. The <u>bacon</u> rested under the shady tree.

2. a. Andrew poured the <u>steak</u> into a glass and served it.

   b. The couple shared a large <u>steak</u> and baked potato for dinner.

3. a. The <u>pork</u> sailed across the ocean to see his friend.

   b. The butcher cut the <u>pork</u> into pieces and made sure to save the ribs for his family.

4. a. The cafeteria serves <u>bologna</u> and cheese sandwiches.

   b. The <u>bologna</u> ate the chicken and fish for dessert.

5. a. <u>Sausages</u> have a long, thin shape.

   b. <u>Sausage</u> is a type of cake.

6. a. Pete put a <u>hotdog</u> in a bun and ate it for lunch.

   b. At the ballpark, the <u>hotdog</u> ran around the bases.

7. a. Strawberries, apples, and <u>ham</u> are types of fruit.

   b. My mother always prepares a baked <u>ham</u> for holiday dinners.

8. a. The price of <u>beef</u> went up, so the family had to eat chicken.

   b. The <u>beef</u> was late, so Margaret went to the store alone.

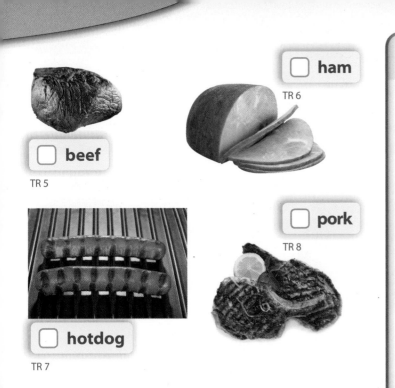

- ☐ ham — TR 6
- ☐ beef — TR 5
- ☐ pork — TR 8
- ☐ hotdog — TR 7

Definitions

Bacon is thin strips of salted or smoked meat that comes from a pig.

Beef is meat from a cow.

Bologna is a type of cooked sausage that is cut into thin pieces and eaten in sandwiches.

Ham is meat from a pig that has been prepared with salt and spices.

A **hotdog** is a small, cooked sausage that is usually served in a bun.

Pork is meat from a pig.

Sausage is a mixture of ground meat and spices.

Steak is a thick, flat piece of beef.

B. Write **T** for **true statements** and **F** for **false statements**.

1. _____ Beef is meat from a cow.

2. _____ Ham is meat from a pig.

3. _____ Bologna and hotdogs are two kinds of ham.

4. _____ A steak is a thick piece of beef.

5. _____ Pork is meat from a chicken.

6. _____ Bacon can be salted or smoked.

7. _____ Sausages are made using only meat.

8. _____ Bologna is a type of cooked pork.

Challenge Words

Check (✔) the words you already know.

- ☐ lard
- ☐ mutton
- ☐ pemmican
- ☐ poultry

153. Candy and Sweets

Check (✔) the words you already know. Then, listen and repeat.

 Tracks 1–23

☐ cake
TR 1

☐ candy
TR 2

☐ cookie
TR 3

☐ cupcake
TR 4

☐ pudding
TR 8

☐ gum
TR 9

☐ pie
TR 10

☐ jam
TR 12

☐ doughnut
TR 13

☐ honey
TR 14

☐ caramel
TR 15

☐ brownie
TR 18

☐ syrup
TR 19

☐ cocoa
TR 20

☐ chocolate
TR 21

☐ butterscotch
TR 22

fudge
TR 5

licorice
TR 6

lollipop
TR 7

marshmallow
TR 11

sherbet
TR 16

sundae
TR 17

vanilla
TR 23

Definitions

A **brownie** is a small, flat, chocolate cake.

Butterscotch is a type of hard brown candy made from butter and sugar.

A **cake** is a sweet food made from flour, eggs, sugar, and butter.

Candy is sweet food such as chocolate or taffy.

Caramel is a type of sweet food made from burnt sugar, butter, and milk.

Chocolate is a sweet brown food that you eat as a sweet or that is used to give flavor to other food.

Cocoa is a brown powder used for making chocolate.

A **cookie** is a small, flat, sweet cake.

A **cupcake** is a small cake for one person.

A **doughnut** is a sweet, round cake with a hole in the middle.

Fudge is soft candy made from butter, sugar, milk, and sometimes chocolate.

Gum is a sweet, sticky substance that you chew for a long time but do not swallow.

Honey is a sweet, sticky food that is made by bees.

Jam is a sweet food that contains soft fruit and sugar.

Licorice is a firm black candy with a strong taste.

A **lollipop** is a hard candy on the end of a stick.

A **marshmallow** is a soft white or pink candy.

A **pie** is a dish of fruit that is covered with pastry and baked.

Pudding is a soft, sweet dessert made from eggs and milk.

Sherbet is a frozen dessert made with fruit juice, sugar, and water.

A **sundae** is a tall glass of ice cream with whipped cream and nuts or fruit on top.

Syrup is a sweet liquid that is made by cooking sugar with water.

Vanilla is a flavor used in sweet food.

49

Check Your Understanding

A. Match each word to the correct description. One description will not be used.

1. _____ pudding
2. _____ jam
3. _____ licorice
4. _____ cupcake
5. _____ lollipop
6. _____ cake
7. _____ sundae
8. _____ doughnut
9. _____ honey
10. _____ pie
11. _____ cocoa
12. _____ sherbet
13. _____ candy
14. _____ gum
15. _____ butterscotch
16. _____ fudge
17. _____ chocolate
18. _____ vanilla
19. _____ cookie
20. _____ marshmallow
21. _____ brownie
22. _____ caramel
23. _____ syrup

a. a sweet food that you make from flour, eggs, sugar, and butter

b. a firm black substance with a strong taste

c. a sweet, sticky substance that you chew but do not swallow

d. soft pink or white candies

e. a sweet, round cake with a hole in the middle

f. a brown powder used to make chocolate

g. sweet food made from burnt sugar, butter, and milk

h. a sweet food that contains soft fruit and sugar

i. a baked dish of fruit covered with pastry

j. a flavor used in sweet food

k. a tall glass of ice cream with whipped cream and fruit or nuts on top

l. sweet liquid made from sugar and water

m. a small, flat, chocolate cake

n. a strong, sharp flavor from the peppermint plant

o. hard brown candy made from butter and sugar

p. a small, flat, sweet cake

q. a soft, sweet dessert made from eggs and milk

r. sweet brown food that you eat as a sweet or that is used to give flavor to other food

s. a hard candy on a stick

t. soft candy made from butter, sugar, milk, and sometimes chocolate

u. a frozen dessert made with fruit, milk, sugar, and water

v. sweet food such as chocolate or taffy

w. a sweet, sticky substance that is made by bees

x. small cake for one person

B. Underline the correct word to complete each sentence.

1. Victor ate the soft, creamy (**pudding / licorice**) with a spoon.

2. Roxy spread the strawberry (**pie / jam**) on her toast for breakfast.

3. Jack chewed on a piece of mint (**gum / doughnut**) to freshen his breath.

4. The birthday (**cake / honey**) had four candles on it.

5. Diane bought a piece of her favorite (**cocoa / candy**), a dark chocolate bar with almonds.

6. Allie loves to eat soft, white (**lollipops / marshmallows**).

7. The small piece of chocolate (**licorice / fudge**) was a special treat.

8. Alvin does not like hard (**butterscotch / marshmallow**) candy.

9. The sugar and water was heated to make (**syrup / sundae**).

10. For dessert, Rick had a (**vanilla / sundae**) covered with whipped cream and nuts.

11. The (**vanilla / sherbet**) ice cream was a perfect choice to make the sundae.

12. Gary ate the small, chocolate (**caramel / brownie**) with a glass of milk.

13. Lily helped her mother bake some chocolate chip (**cookies / jams**).

14. (**Honey / Gum**) is made by bees.

15. Tanya brought small, frosted (**vanilla / cupcakes**) for all twelve guests.

16. The chewy, sticky (**caramel / lollipop**) candy was covered with chocolate.

17. Andrea enjoyed a bowl of cold (**doughnut / sherbet**) on the hot summer day.

18. (**Sundaes / Doughnuts**) are shaped like the letter O.

19. Francis cut the peach (**pie / pudding**) in slices for each of his friends.

20. (**Chocolate / Pie**) is used to flavor many foods, such as candy, milk, cake, and even cereal.

21. Not many children like the (**cake / licorice**) candies because the flavor is too strong.

22. (**Caramel / Cocoa**) is used for making chocolate.

23. When Alex was finished eating the (**lollipop / syrup**), he put the stick in the trash can.

Challenge Words

Check (✔) the words you already know.

- [ ] lozenge
- [ ] marmalade
- [ ] pastry
- [ ] peppermint
- [ ] shortcake
- [ ] spearmint
- [ ] tart
- [ ] toffee

162. Food-Related Actions

Check (✔) the words you already know. Then, listen and repeat.

Tracks 1–9

☐ **bake**

TR 1

☐ **boil**

TR 2

☐ **serve**

TR 3

☐ **fry**

TR 4

☐ **roast**

TR 5

☐ **cook**

TR 6

Definitions

When you **bake** food, you cook it in an oven.

If you **barbecue** food, you cook it over an open fire, usually outside.

When you **boil** food, you cook it in a liquid that has been heated to 212° F or 100° C.

When you **broil** food, you cook it using very strong heat directly above it.

When you **cook** a meal, you prepare and heat food.

When you **fry** food, you cook it in hot fat or oil.

When you **grill** food, you cook it on metal bars over a fire.

When you **roast** meat or other food, you cook it at a high temperature in an oven or over a fire.

When you **serve** food and drinks, you give people food and drinks.

☐ **broil**

TR 7

☐ **grill**

TR 8

☐ **barbecue**

TR 9

53

Check Your Understanding

A. Match each word to the correct description. One description will not be used.

1. _____ roast
2. _____ barbecue
3. _____ serve
4. _____ grill
5. _____ broil
6. _____ fry
7. _____ boil
8. _____ bake
9. _____ cook

a. to cook food in an oven

b. to cook food in hot fat or oil

c. to give people food or drinks

d. to cook over an open fire

e. to cook food on metal bars above a fire

f. to cook food at a high temperature in an oven or over a fire

g. to cook food using very strong heat directly above it

h. to cook food in liquid that has been heated to 212ºF

i. to press and stretch a mixture with your hands to make it smooth

j. to prepare and heat food

B. Underline the correct word to complete each sentence.

1. Every Sunday, she (**fries / bakes**) a chocolate cake in the oven.

2. (**Boil / Barbecue**) the egg in the water for three minutes.

3. My aunt asked me to (**serve / fry**) the lemonade to the guests.

4. It's time to (**fry / grill**) the corn over the fire.

5. She put two steaks in the hot oven to (**broil / boil**).

6. Jane and her husband enjoy (**cooking / roasting**) soups and stews.

7. For Thanksgiving dinner, my mother (**grilled / roasted**) a turkey in the oven.

8. Paul (**fried / broiled**) bacon and two eggs in hot fat for his breakfast.

9. Richard had a Fourth of July party and (**boiled / barbecued**) steaks and hamburgers for everyone outside over a fire.

Challenge Words

Check (✔) the words you already know.

☐ brew   ☐ deteriorate   ☐ scald   ☐ simmer

☐ cookout   ☐ knead   ☐ sift   ☐ spoil

174. Fruits

Check (✔) the words you already know. Then, listen and repeat.

 Tracks 1–21

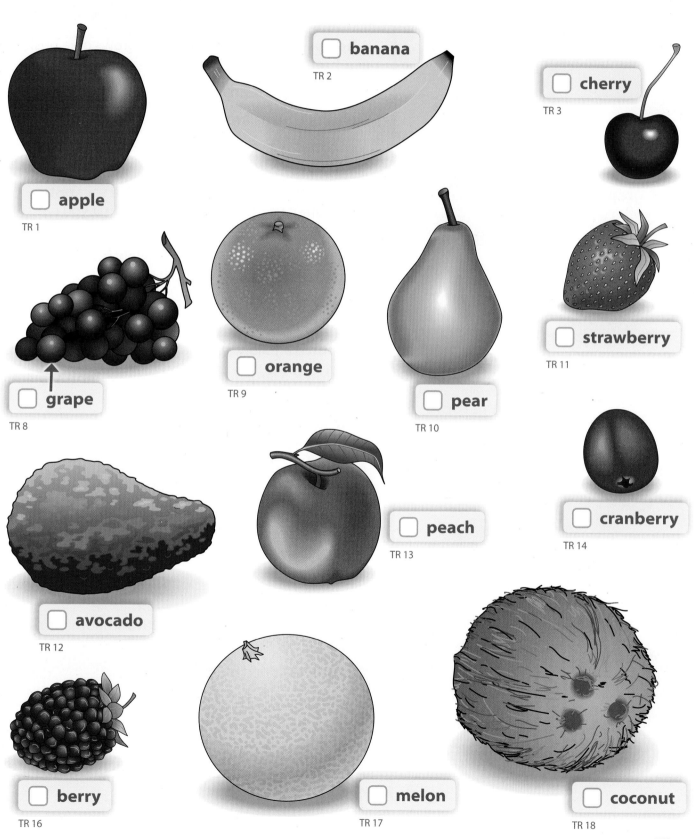

☐ **banana**
TR 2

☐ **cherry**
TR 3

☐ **apple**
TR 1

☐ **grape**
TR 8

☐ **orange**
TR 9

☐ **pear**
TR 10

☐ **strawberry**
TR 11

☐ **avocado**
TR 12

☐ **peach**
TR 13

☐ **cranberry**
TR 14

☐ **berry**
TR 16

☐ **melon**
TR 17

☐ **coconut**
TR 18

lemon

TR 4

blueberry

TR 5

grapefruit

TR 6

plum

TR 7

pineapple

TR 15

raspberry

TR 20

prune

TR 19

raisin

TR 21

Definitions

An **apple** is a firm, round fruit with green, red, or yellow skin.

An **avocado** is a fruit with dark green skin and a large seed in the middle.

A **banana** is a long, curved fruit with yellow skin.

A **berry** is a small, round fruit that grows on a bush or a tree.

A **blueberry** is a small, dark blue fruit.

A **cherry** is a small, round fruit with red skin.

A **coconut** is a very large nut with a hairy shell that grows on trees in warm countries.

A **cranberry** is a small, red fruit with a sour taste, that is often used for making a sauce that you eat with meat.

A **grapefruit** is a large, round, yellow fruit that has a slightly sour taste.

A **grape** is a small green or purple fruit that grows in bunches.

A **lemon** is a yellow fruit with very sour juice.

A **melon** is a large fruit with soft, sweet flesh and a hard green or yellow skin.

An **orange** is a round, juicy fruit with a thick, orange-colored skin.

A **peach** is a round fruit with a soft red and orange skin.

A **pear** is a juicy fruit that is narrow at the top and wider at the bottom. Pears have white flesh and green, yellow, or brown skin.

A **pineapple** is a large fruit with sweet yellow flesh and thick brown skin.

A **plum** is a small, sweet fruit with a smooth purple, red, or yellow skin and a seed in the middle.

A **prune** is a dried plum.

A **raisin** is a dried grape.

A **raspberry** is a small, soft, red fruit that grows on a bush.

A **strawberry** is a small, soft, red fruit that has a lot of very small seeds on its skin.

Check Your Understanding

A. Write **T** for **true sentences** and **F** for **false sentences**.

1. _____ Raspberries grow on bushes.

2. _____ Cherries are a long, curved red fruit.

3. _____ Bananas have yellow skin.

4. _____ Peaches have red and orange skin.

5. _____ Berries are small fruits.

6. _____ Grapes grow in bunches.

7. _____ Melons have very soft green or yellow skin.

8. _____ Strawberries are small and red and have seeds inside.

9. _____ Plums have bumpy purple, red, or yellow skin.

10. _____ Oranges have thick skin.

11. _____ Blueberries have hairy shells.

12. _____ Pears have a round shape.

13. _____ Grapefruits have a sweet taste.

14. _____ Cranberries can be used to make sauce that you eat with meat.

15. _____ Apples can be yellow, red, or green on the outside.

16. _____ Raisins are made from grapes.

17. _____ Pineapples are a kind of yellow apple.

18. _____ A prune is a dried pineapple.

19. _____ Coconuts grow in warm countries.

20. _____ Lemons are a juicy, sour fruit.

21. _____ An avocado has small seeds inside.

B. Underline the word that correctly completes each sentence.

1. We picked (**cherries / melons**) from a tree.

2. The (**avocadoes / raspberries**) were juicy and sweet to eat.

3. One type of berry is a (**prune / strawberry**).

4. Nancy ate a red (**plum / grapefruit**) for a healthy snack.

5. The (**cranberry / banana**) sauce tasted sour, so I added more sugar as it was cooking.

6. A dry plum is called a (**raisin / prune**).

7. We squeezed (**avocadoes / oranges**) to make juice.

8. Grapes that are dried are called (**raisins / grapefruits**).

9. A strawberry is a type of (**peach / berry**).

10. An (**avocado / apple**) has a large seed inside of it.

11. (**Pears / Strawberries**) are a juicy fruit that is wider at the bottom than at the top.

12. Jessica picked up a (**peach / coconut**) to feel its soft skin.

13. Mom says not to pick the (**bananas / blueberries**) until they are a deep blue color.

14. The (**cherry / melon**) was so large that I needed both hands to carry it.

15. The (**grapefruit / pineapple**) tasted a little sour to Natalia.

16. Gregory peeled the yellow skins from the (**strawberries / bananas**) before slicing them.

17. (**Pears / Grapes**) can be green or purple.

18. You have to cut through the thick, brown skin of the (**raspberry / pineapple**) if you want to eat the fruit.

19. Melanie needed some sour fruit juice for the recipe, so she was disappointed to see that the store didn't have any (**lemons / peaches**).

20. (**Apples / Cranberries**) can be green, yellow, or red.

21. The shell of the (**avocado / coconut**) was so hard, it was hard to break open.

Challenge Words

Check (✔) the words you already know.

- [ ] applesauce
- [ ] apricot
- [ ] fig
- [ ] honeydew
- [ ] lime
- [ ] tangerine
- [ ] watermelon

176. Drinks

Check (✔) the words you already know. Then, listen and repeat.

Tracks 1–11

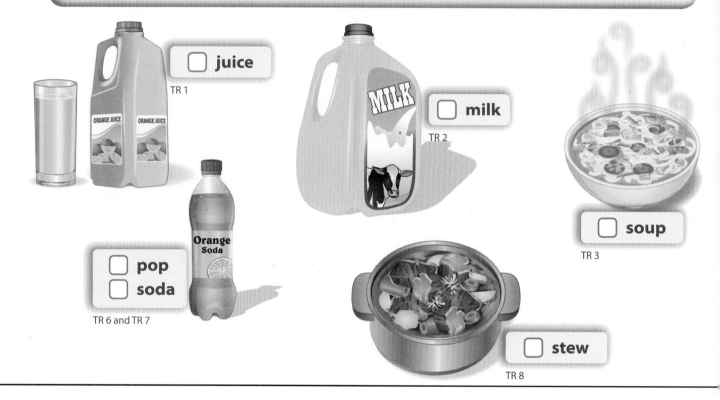

☐ juice
TR 1

☐ milk
TR 2

☐ soup
TR 3

☐ pop
☐ soda
TR 6 and TR 7

☐ stew
TR 8

Check Your Understanding

A. Choose the sentence that correctly uses the underlined word.

1. a. Reggie ordered a glass of orange <u>juice</u> with his breakfast.

   b. Margaret cut the <u>juice</u> into five slices.

2. a. The hot lemon <u>tea</u> helped the sick girl's throat feel better.

   b. The <u>tea</u> was mixed with powder to make building blocks.

3. a. Diana had never tasted fresh <u>milk</u> from a cow.

   b. They gathered the ripe <u>milk</u> from the giant green trees.

4. a. The angry <u>wine</u> chased the cat around the table.

   b. <u>Wine</u> is made from grapes.

5. a. Mom made a huge pot of beef <u>stew</u> for the dinner party.

   b. Zachary dipped his feet in the warm <u>stew</u>.

Definitions

Beer is an alcoholic drink made from grain.

Chili is a food made with beans and meat in a hot, spicy sauce made with chili powder.

Coffee is a dark brown drink made by brewing ground-up coffee beans and adding hot water.

Juice is the liquid from a fruit or vegetable.

Milk is the white liquid that cows and some other animals produce which people drink.

Pop is another word for *soda*.

Soda is a sweet, bubbly drink.

Soup is liquid food made by boiling meat, fish, or vegetables in water.

A **stew** is a thick soup made by cooking meat, vegetables, and liquid for a long period of time.

Tea is a drink that you make by pouring boiling water over the dry leaves of a plant.

Wine is an alcoholic drink made from grapes.

6. a. Jim enjoyed his cup of <u>coffee</u> with a little milk and sugar.

   b. <u>Coffee</u> is a fantastic flying brown animal.

7. a. The teenager ordered a bottle of grape <u>pop</u> with lunch.

   b. At lunch, the <u>pop</u> was served on a plate with butter.

8. a. Emma poured <u>soup</u> on the sponge and washed the dishes.

   b. The cup of tomato <u>soup</u> was too hot for Eric to eat.

9. a. Wendy liked her <u>soda</u> grilled until it was dark brown.

   b. I like to order my <u>soda</u> with extra ice.

10. a. Tom ate a bowl of hot <u>chili</u>.

    b. Olga filled the washing machine with clothes and <u>chili</u>.

11. a. The <u>beer</u> joined the singing bird in the tree.

    b. The bar served <u>beer</u> to adults only.

B. Choose the correct word from the word bank to complete each sentence. One word will not be used.

tea	**pop**	**soda**	**soup**
chili	**milk**	**juice**	**stew**
beer	**broth**	**coffee**	**wine**

1. Rita squeezed a few oranges to make fresh _____ for breakfast.

2. The vegetable _____ had carrots, potatoes, and corn in it.

3. Norah poured some cold, white _____ in her coffee and stirred it with a spoon.

4. At the restaurant, Bill and Jane ordered steaks and two glasses of red _____ with dinner.

5. _____ is another word for *soda*.

6. Even though Scott used a small amount of chili powder in his pot of _____ , his friends thought it was too spicy.

7. Sandy drank a can of orange _____ with her lunch.

8. Teresa's guests didn't want coffee, so she offered them cups of hot _____ instead.

9. My mother doesn't drink alcohol, but my father sometimes drinks a _____ with his dinner.

10. The thick _____ contained beef, potatoes, and carrots.

11. Each morning, Betty grinds beans and boils water to make fresh _____ .

Challenge Words

Check (✔) the words you already know.

☐ alcohol   ☐ broth   ☐ cider

☐ beverage   ☐ champagne   ☐ liquor

62

208. Vegetables, Grains, and Nuts

Check (✔) the words you already know. Then, listen and repeat.

☐ **almond**
TR 1

☐ **bean**
TR 2

☐ **carrot**
TR 3

☐ **lettuce**
TR 5

☐ **cashew**
TR 4

Definitions

An **almond** is a sweet-flavored nut that you can eat or use in cooking.

A **bean** is a seed from a plant that can be eaten.

A **carrot** is a long, thin, orange-colored vegetable.

A **cashew** is a curved nut that you can eat.

Celery is a vegetable that consists of long, pale-green sticks.

Corn is a tall, green plant with large, yellow seeds on long ears that is fed to cattle or is cooked and eaten by people.

A **cucumber** is a long, dark-green vegetable with crisp, white flesh.

Lettuce is a plant with large green or red leaves that is eaten mainly in salads.

A **nut** is a small fruit with a hard shell.

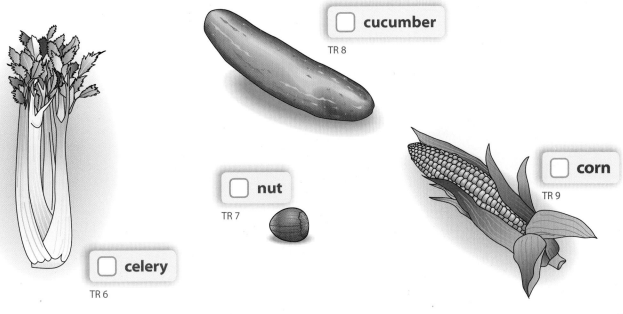

☐ **cucumber**
TR 8

☐ **corn**
TR 9

☐ **nut**
TR 7

☐ **celery**
TR 6

☐ **peas**

TR 10

☐ **spinach**

TR 11

☐ **pickle**

TR 14

☐ **squash**

TR 15

☐ **tomato**

TR 16

☐ **pumpkin**

TR 19

☐ **popcorn**

TR 20

☐ **rice**

TR 22

☐ **potato**

TR 23

olive

TR 12

onion

TR 13

peanut

TR 17

wheat

TR 18

walnut

TR 21

seed

TR 24

Definitions

An **olive** is a small green or black fruit that grows on trees and can be eaten or can be used to make oil.

An **onion** is a round vegetable with many layers. It has a strong, sharp smell and taste.

A **peanut** is a small, light-brown nut about the size of a pea, that grows underground and is a popular snack food.

Peas are small, round, green seeds that grow in long pods and are eaten as a vegetable.

A **pickle** is a small cucumber soaked in vinegar and spices.

Popcorn is a type of food that consists of kernels of corn that have been heated until they have burst and become large and light.

A **potato** is a hard, round, white vegetable with brown or red skin. A potato grows under the ground.

A **pumpkin** is a large, round, orange vegetable with a hard, thick skin and soft flesh.

Rice is white or brown grains from a plant that grows in wet areas.

A **seed** is the small, hard part of a plant from which a new plant grows.

Spinach is a dark green vegetable with large leaves.

A **squash** is a large vegetable with a hard or firm skin.

A **tomato** is a soft, red fruit that you can eat raw in salads or cook like a vegetable.

A **walnut** is a nut that is hard and round with a rough texture.

Wheat is a crop that is grown for food. It is made into flour and used for making bread.

Check Your Understanding

A. Write each word in the correct column.

onion	pickle	squash	potato
rice	peas	popcorn	seed
peanut	nut	celery	wheat
tomato	lettuce	walnut	bean
carrot	almond	cashew	spinach
cucumber	olive	corn	pumpkin

VEGETABLES	GRAINS	NUTS	FRUITS	OTHER

B. Underline the correct word to complete each sentence.

1. Tim washed tomatoes, cucumbers, and green leafy (**lettuce / pickle**) to make a delicious salad.

2. The baker needed two cups of (**wheat / tomato**) to make the bread.

3. To eat the (**celery / walnut**), Betty had to crack the hard, rough shell.

4. The baked (**potato / cucumber**) was delicious with butter and salt.

5. She ate a large slice of (**popcorn / pumpkin**) pie for dessert.

6. Dan loved to eat white (**rice / lettuce**) and beans mixed together.

7. The large, green leaves of (**spinach / peanut**) are full of vitamins and minerals.

8. After cutting the thick-skinned (**rice / squash**) into pieces, Chris added them to the other vegetables in the soup.

9. The juicy, red (**tomato / olive**) was sliced and put on the hamburger.

10. The children planted the (**seed / popcorn**) in the ground and watered it.

11. I'm allergic to nuts, so please don't put (**onions / almonds**) in the cookies.

12. The store sold red, black, and white (**beans / cucumbers**).

13. A (**cashew / celery**) is a curved nut.

14. At this diner, they serve many sandwiches with a (**pea / pickle**).

15. The (**pea / tomato**) soup had an attractive bright green color.

16. The many layers of the (**onion / carrot**) were peeled off one at a time.

17. Marvin's mother served a bowl full of black and green (**olives / peanuts**) before dinner.

18. The long, dark-green (**cucumber / tomato**) was sliced and added to the salad.

19. I wanted a crunchy snack, so I chose a bowl of (**tomato / celery**) sticks.

20. The rabbit nibbled on the orange (**carrot / pickle**).

21. Steve's favorite (**grain / nut**) is the almond.

22. Marta and Betty ate a bowl of (**popcorn / wheat**) as they watched a movie.

23. At the ballgame, Roger bought a bag of salted (**peanuts / beans**) for a snack.

24. The family peeled the green leaves back to reveal the yellow (**corn / potato**) inside.

Challenge Words

Check (✔) the words you already know.

- ☐ asparagus
- ☐ cabbage
- ☐ cauliflower
- ☐ eggplant
- ☐ maize
- ☐ radish
- ☐ turnip
- ☐ yam

222. Tastes Related to Food

Check (✔) the words you already know. Then, listen and repeat.

 Tracks 1–7

☐ **taste**

TR 1

☐ **flavor**

TR 2

Definitions

The **flavor** of a food or drink is its taste.

If food is **juicy**, it has a lot of juice in it.

Ripe fruit or grain is ready to eat.

Something that is **sour** has a sharp taste like the taste of a lemon.

Sweet food and drink contains a lot of sugar.

The **taste** of something is the sweet, sour, bitter, or salty quality that it has when you put it in your mouth.

If food is **tasty,** it has a pleasant flavor and is good to eat.

☐ **juicy**

TR 3

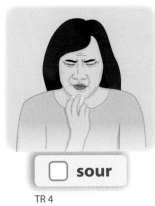

☐ **sour**

TR 4

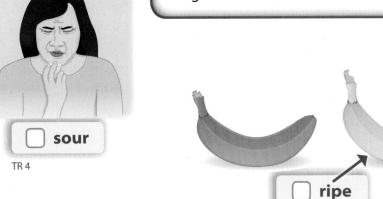

☐ **ripe**

TR 5

☐ **sweet**

TR 6

☐ **tasty**

TR 7

Check Your Understanding

A. Match each word to the correct description. One description will not be used.

1. _____ tasty
2. _____ sour
3. _____ juicy
4. _____ taste
5. _____ flavor
6. _____ ripe
7. _____ sweet

a. when food or drink has a lot of sugar

b. when food has a pleasant flavor and is good to eat

c. when food is no longer fresh

d. when fruit or grain is ready to eat

e. when food has a lot of juice

f. the taste of a food or drink

g. the particular quality a food or drink has when you put it in your mouth

h. when something has a sharp flavor

B. Choose the sentence that correctly uses the underlined word.

1. a. The couple loved the <u>flavor</u> of the ice cream, so they ordered another scoop.

   b. The <u>flavor</u> was upset over the decision.

2. a. The popcorn had a salty yet sweet <u>taste</u>.

   b. The <u>taste</u> was locked in the cage with the other big cats.

3. a. The dried leather was <u>juicy</u> and brown.

   b. The tomato was so <u>juicy</u> that when cut open, juice dripped on the table.

4. a. The cow was <u>ripe</u>, so the farmer put him in the barn.

   b. It was time to pick the apples because they were <u>ripe</u>.

5. a. The baby made a funny face as he bit into the <u>sour</u> lemon.

   b. The <u>sour</u> auto used diesel fuel.

6. a. After tasting the coffee, Casey thought it was <u>sweet</u> enough, so he did not add more sugar.

   b. He used the <u>sweet</u> paper to write his school report on.

7. a. Isabel felt <u>tasty</u> after eating too much pasta.

   b. The pizza was so <u>tasty</u> that I decided to eat a second slice.

Challenge Words

Check (✔) the words you already know.

☐ bitter   ☐ edible   ☐ stale   ☐ tangy

☐ delicious   ☐ savor   ☐ succulent

232. Hunger and Thirst

Check (✔) the words you already know. Then, listen and repeat.

Tracks 1–5

☐ **starve**

TR 1

Definitions

When you are **hungry**, you want to eat.

Hunger is the feeling that you need to eat.

To **starve** means to feel pain or to die from lack of food.

Thirst is the feeling that you need to drink something.

When you are **thirsty**, you want to drink something.

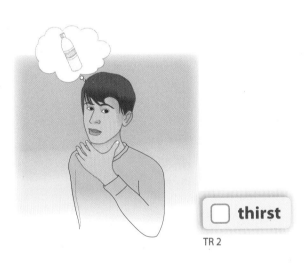

☐ **thirst**

TR 2

☐ **thirsty**

TR 3

☐ **hungry**

TR 4

☐ **hunger**

TR 5

Check Your Understanding

A. Underline the correct word to complete each sentence.

1. To satisfy her (**thirst / thirsty**), Tina drank several glasses of water.

2. The (**hunger / hungry**) baby cried until he got his bottle of milk.

3. Many people in the village (**starved / thirst**) when their crops were destroyed.

4. Rhonda became (**thirst / thirsty**) when she hiked in the desert.

5. Bill started to feel weak from (**hunger / hungry**), so he knew it was time to eat lunch.

B. Choose the correct word from the box to complete each sentence. One word will not be used.

thirst	starve	thirsty
hungry	appetite	hunger

1. Some people _____ because they do not have money for food.

2. People normally experience _____ after they spend time outside on a hot day.

3. She was _____ all morning because she didn't eat anything for breakfast.

4. I was so _____ that I drank a full bottle of water without stopping.

5. To satisfy his _____, Steven ate two servings for dinner.

Challenge Words

Check (✔) the word if you already know it.

☐ appetite

246. Types of Food

Check (✔) the words you already know. Then, listen and repeat.

Tracks 1–7

☐ **food**
TR 1

☐ **crop**
TR 2

Definitions

A **crop** is a plant that people grow for food.

Food is what people and animals eat.

Fruit is a usually sweet food that grows on a tree or a plant.

Meat is the part of an animal that people use for food.

Seafood is fish and shellfish that live in the ocean and are used for food.

Sweets are foods that contain a lot of sugar and taste sweet.

Vegetables are plants or parts of plants that you can eat.

☐ **fruit**
TR 3

☐ **meat**
TR 4

☐ **seafood**
TR 5

☐ **sweets**
TR 6

☐ **vegetables**
TR 7

Check Your Understanding

A. Match each word to the correct description. One description will not be used.

1. _____ seafood
2. _____ vegetables
3. _____ meat
4. _____ fruit
5. _____ sweets
6. _____ crop
7. _____ food

a. plants or parts of plants that people eat
b. fish and other ocean animals that people eat
c. what people and animals eat
d. the part of an animal that people eat
e. units that measure how much energy is in food
f. a sweet food that grows on a tree or bush
g. foods that contain a lot of sugar
h. a plant that people grow for food

B. Choose the sentence that correctly uses the underlined word.

1. a. The <u>vegetables</u> are swimming in the lake.

   b. The soup was made from only <u>vegetables</u> and did not have any meat in it.

2. a. My grandmother has a garden where she grows many kinds of <u>sweets</u>.

   b. The little boy looked at all the <u>sweets</u>, and then he chose a chocolate bar with almonds.

3. a. The fishermen worked all day on their boats to catch <u>seafood</u> for their families.

   b. The <u>seafood</u> grew in the middle of the desert where there is little water.

4. a. The shark searched for <u>fruit</u> inside the underwater cave.

   b. I like all <u>fruit</u>, but my favorite fruit is pineapple.

5. a. The farmer noticed that the <u>crop</u> of corn was dry, so he watered it.

   b. The <u>crop</u> pulled out of the parking space and drove down the bumpy road.

6. a. Airplanes and cars are types of <u>food</u>.

   b. Vegetables and fruits are types of <u>food</u>.

7. a. The tender, juicy <u>meat</u> came from a cow.

   b. The <u>meat</u> was from the leaves of the tall orange trees.

Challenge Words

Check (✔) the words you already know.

- [ ] calorie
- [ ] carbohydrate
- [ ] diet
- [ ] legume
- [ ] nourishment
- [ ] nutrient
- [ ] nutrition
- [ ] protein

53. Poems and Songs

Check (✔) the words you already know. Then, listen and repeat.

Tracks 1–6

☐ **song**

TR 1

Definitions

A **hymn** is a religious song of praise.

A **lullaby** is a quiet song that is sung to children to help them to go to sleep.

Music is the pleasant sound that you make when you sing or play instruments.

A **poem** is a piece of writing in which the words are chosen for their beauty and sound, and are carefully arranged, often in short lines.

A **rhyme** is a poem that has words that sound alike at the end of its lines.

A **song** is words and music sung together.

☐ **lullaby**

TR 2

☐ **poem**

TR 3

Battle Hymn of the Republic

☐ **hymn**

TR 4

☐ **music**

TR 5

☐ **rhyme**

TR 6

Check Your Understanding

A. Match each word to the correct description. One description will not be used.

1. _____ lullaby
2. _____ music
3. _____ poem
4. _____ rhyme
5. _____ song
6. _____ hymn

   a. a poem that has words that sound alike

   b. a religious song of praise

   c. a quiet song that is sung to children

   d. a song sung during Christmastime

   e. the pleasant sound that you make when you sing or play instruments

   f. a combination of words and music

   g. a piece of writing with short lines and carefully chosen words

B. Circle the word that could replace the underlined phrase in the sentence without changing its meaning.

1. Andrew enjoys listening to <u>pleasant sounds made by voices and instruments</u>.

   a. lullaby   b. music   c. hymn

2. Janet needed to learn the <u>words and music sung together</u> for her class performance.

   a. rhyme   b. poem   c. song

3. The mother sang a <u>gentle song</u> while she rocked her baby to sleep.

   a. lullaby   b. rhyme   c. hymn

4. While the organ played the music, the people sang a <u>religious song</u>.

   a. rhyme   b. hymn   c. poem

5. After the poet read his <u>piece of writing arranged in short lines</u>, everyone applauded.

   a. poem   b. song   c. music

6. Elizabeth spent many hours trying to finish the <u>poem with ending words for each line that sound alike</u>.

   a. lullaby   b. rhyme   c. song

Challenge Words

Check (✔) the words you already know.

- [ ] ballad
- [ ] carol
- [ ] ditty
- [ ] limerick
- [ ] lyric
- [ ] measure
- [ ] meter
- [ ] stanza

71. Writing, Drawing, and Reading

Check (✔) the words you already know. Then, listen and repeat.

Tracks 1–16

☐ **color**
TR 1

☐ **skim**
TR 2

☐ **draw**
TR 3

☐ **paint**
TR 4

☐ **print**
TR 6

☐ **scribble**
TR 7

☐ **write**
TR 8

☐ **read**
TR 10

☐ **handwriting**
TR 11

☐ **sign**
TR 12

☐ **misspell**
TR 13

☐ **underline**
TR 14

☐ **trace**
TR 15

Spelling Bee

S-U-N-R-I-S-E

☐ spell

TR 5

☐ publish

TR 9

☐ copy

TR 16

Definitions

To **color** something means to add color to it by using pens, crayons, markers, or pencils.

To **copy** something means to make or write something that is exactly like original thing.

To **draw** means to use a pencil or pen to make a picture.

Your **handwriting** is your style of writing with a pen or a pencil.

To **misspell** means to spell a word incorrectly.

To **paint** means to create a picture or work of art using paint.

To **print** means to write letters that are not joined together.

To **publish** a book, a magazine, or a newspaper means to prepare and print copies of it.

To **read** a book or a story means to look at the written words and understand them.

To **scribble** something means to write or draw it quickly and roughly.

To **sign** a document means to write your name on it.

To **skim** a piece of writing or to skim through something means to read through it or look over it quickly.

To **spell** means to write or speak each letter in a word in the correct order.

To **trace** a picture means to make a copy of it by covering it with a piece of transparent paper and drawing over the lines underneath.

To **underline** a word or a sentence means to draw a line under it.

To **write** means to use a pen, a pencil, or a computer to produce words, letters, or numbers.

Check Your Understanding

A. Match each word to the correct description. One description will not be used.

1. _____ read
2. _____ print
3. _____ copy
4. _____ color
5. _____ write
6. _____ underline
7. _____ spell
8. _____ misspell
9. _____ sign
10. _____ publish
11. _____ draw
12. _____ scribble
13. _____ handwriting
14. _____ skim
15. _____ trace
16. _____ paint

a. to write or speak each letter in the correct order

b. to create a book, poem, or piece of music

c. to write the short form of a word or phrase

d. a particular way of writing with pen or pencil

e. to make something exactly like the original

f. to copy on transparent paper using an image underneath

g. to use a pencil or pen to make a picture

h. to prepare and print copies of writing

i. to add color to a picture

j. to draw a line under something

k. to write in letters that are not connected

l. to write your name on a document

m. to make a picture using paint

n. to look at written words and understand them

o. to read through something very quickly

p. to write quickly and roughly

q. to not spell correctly

B. Circle the word that could replace the underlined phrase in the sentence without changing its meaning.

1. Karen was careful not to <u>incorrectly spell</u> any words on the report.

   a. misspell   b. copy   c. color

2. The doctor <u>wrote his name on</u> the prescription.

   a. signed   b. paint   c. traced

3. Andy learned how to <u>quickly read</u> a text so that he could understand the main ideas.

   a. handwriting   b. skim   c. scribble

4. The company was ready to <u>prepare and print copies of</u> the author's next book.

   a. sign   b. misspell   c. publish

5. Tyler was learning to <u>write in letters that are not joined together</u> in his first grade class.

    a. underlined   b. print   c. publish

6. During Teresa's art class, she <u>used paint to produce</u> a bowl of fruit.

    a. painted   b. spelled   c. traced

7. Lauren's father is an artist. He taught her how to <u>use a pencil or pen to make a picture</u>.

    a. skim   b. spell   c. draw

8. Peter's <u>style of writing with a pen</u> was so neat and clear that he won an award for it.

    a. handwriting   b. draw   c. underline

9. Gary managed to <u>write in the correct order</u> every word on his test.

    a. misspell   b. spell   c. sign

10. Before going shopping, she <u>wrote something that is exactly like the original</u> the list of ingredients needed to bake a coconut cake.

    a. read   b. copied   c. skimmed

11. Ben <u>quickly wrote</u> some notes, while his teacher continued to lecture.

    a. scribbled   b. painted   c. drew

12. The students <u>created, prepared, and printed</u> the monthly school newspaper.

    a. published   b. painted   c. read

13. To learn to print the alphabet, Mary <u>copied by writing over</u> the letters in her workbook.

    a. scribbled   b. traced   c. underlined

14. David <u>added color to</u> the maps for his geography class.

    a. colored   b. read   c. printed

15. Paul <u>drew a line below</u> certain words in his book that seemed important.

    a. drew   b. underlined   c. signed

16. Some children can <u>look at and understand written words</u> when they are very young.

    a. color   b. trace   c. read

Challenge Words

Check (✔) the words you already know.

☐ abbreviate   ☐ draft   ☐ indent   ☐ proofread

☐ doodle   ☐ illustrate   ☐ legible   ☐ rewrite

112. Things to Write On / With

Check (✔) the words you already know. Then, listen and repeat.

Tracks 1–14

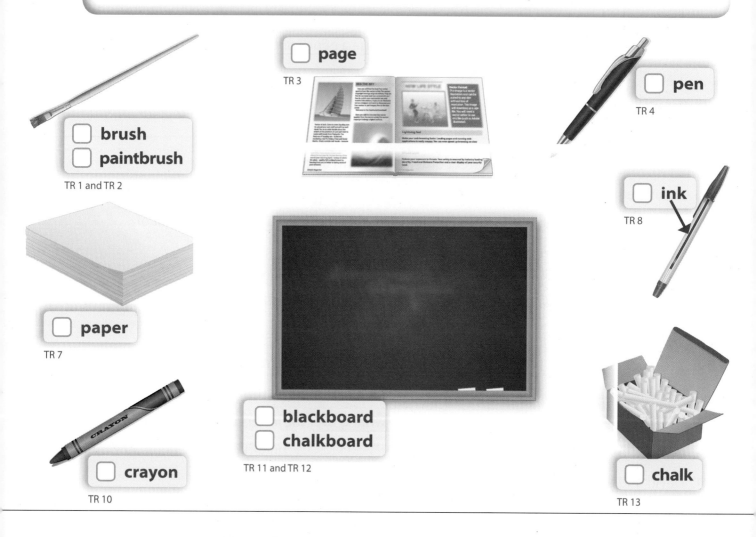

- ☐ **page**
  TR 3

- ☐ **pen**
  TR 4

- ☐ **brush**
- ☐ **paintbrush**
  TR 1 and TR 2

- ☐ **ink**
  TR 8

- ☐ **paper**
  TR 7

- ☐ **blackboard**
- ☐ **chalkboard**
  TR 11 and TR 12

- ☐ **crayon**
  TR 10

- ☐ **chalk**
  TR 13

Check Your Understanding

A. Circle the word that correctly completes each sentence.

1. Susie used a blue _____ to add color to the sky in her drawing.

   a. blackboard   b. page   c. crayon

2. Sean filled up all the pages in his _____ with writings and drawings.

   a. notebook   b. card   c. ink

3. The teacher wrote a sentence on the _____ for the whole class to read.

   a. pen   b. chalk   c. chalkboard

4. Ted put 15 new pages of paper in his _____ notebook.

   a. loose-leaf   b. brush   c. pencil

☐ pencil
TR 5

☐ card
TR 6

☐ loose-leaf
TR 9

☐ notebook
TR 14

Definitions

A **blackboard** is a big, dark-colored board for writing on in a classroom.

A **brush** is an object that has a lot of bristles or hairs attached to it. You use a brush for painting.

A **card** is a piece of stiff paper with a picture and a message that you send to someone on a special occasion.

Chalk is small sticks of soft, white, powdery substance that you use for writing or drawing.

A **chalkboard** is a dark-colored board that you write on with chalk.

A **crayon** is a small, colored stick of wax that you use for drawing or coloring.

Ink is the colored liquid found in pens and used for writing.

A **loose-leaf** notebook is a hardcover notebook that contains paper that you can easily remove.

A **notebook** is a small book for writing notes in.

A **page** is one side of a piece of paper in a book, a magazine, or a newspaper.

A **paintbrush** is a brush that you use for painting.

Paper is a material that you write on.

A **pen** is a long, thin object that you use for writing with ink.

A **pencil** is a thin piece of wood with a black or colored substance through the middle that you use to write or draw with.

5. In her book bag, Jessica always carries four sharpened _____ .

   a. inks   b. pencils

   c. pages

6. Natalia used _____ to write on the blackboard.

   a. chalk   b. paintbrushes   c. notebook

7. Pens are filled with _____ .

   a. paper   b. ink   c. card

8. After Mindy was done painting, she washed her hands and cleaned the _____ .

   a. paintbrushes   b. pen   c. card

9. Another word for *chalkboard* is _____ .

    a. loose-leaf   b. blackboard   c. chalk

10. Joe made his grandfather a birthday _____ .

    a. brush   b. crayon   c. card

11. Patricia always carries a few _____ in her purse in case she needs to write down something.

    a. pens   b. chalk   c. ink

12. On the first _____ of his journal, Tom wrote about his first day at school.

    a. notebook   b. page   c. pencil

13. What kind of _____ do you need for painting?

    a. chalkboard   b. pen   c. brush

14. Isaac needed to borrow a piece of _____ to write some notes.

    a. crayon   b. blackboard   c. paper

B. Write each word from the word bank in the correct column.

ink	paper	page	pen	brush
notebook	crayon	chalk	card	blackboard
chalkboard	paintbrush	pencil	loose-leaf	

ITEMS YOU WRITE OR DRAW WITH	ITEMS YOU WRITE OR DRAW ON/IN

Challenge Words

Check (✔) the words you already know.

☐ ballpoint   ☐ pastel   ☐ ream   ☐ scroll   ☐ typewriter

☐ parchment   ☐ press   ☐ scrapbook   ☐ tablet

138. Literature (Types)

Check (✔) the words you already know. Then, listen and repeat.

 Tracks 1–10

☐ **story**
TR 2

☐ **myth**
TR 1

Definitions

Fiction is books and stories about people and events that are not real.

A **legend** is a very old and popular story.

Literature is books, plays, and poetry that most people consider to be of high quality.

A **mystery** is a story about a crime or strange events that are only explained at the end.

A **myth** is an ancient story about history, gods, or heroes.

Poetry is the form of literature that consists of poems.

A **riddle** is a question that seems to be nonsense but that has a clever answer.

A **story** is a description of imaginary people and events that is intended to entertain people.

A **tale** is a story.

Writing is something that has been written or printed.

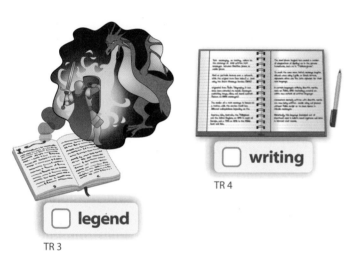

☐ **writing**
TR 4

☐ **legend**
TR 3

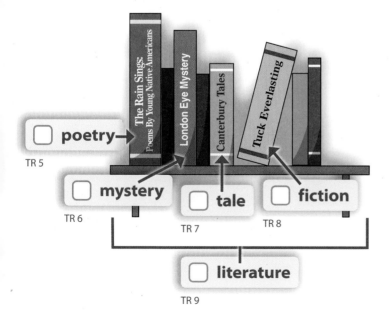

☐ **poetry**
TR 5

☐ **mystery**
TR 6

☐ **tale**
TR 7

☐ **fiction**
TR 8

☐ **literature**
TR 9

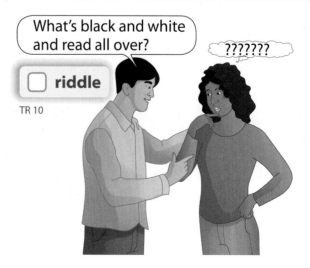

What's black and white and read all over?

???????

☐ **riddle**
TR 10

Check Your Understanding

A. Match each word to the correct description. One description will not be used.

1. _____ mystery   a. a very old and popular story

2. _____ literature   b. a short sentence that gives advice or tells you something about life

3. _____ fiction   c. a question that seems to be nonsense but that has a clever answer

4. _____ legend   d. books and stories about people and events that are not real

5. _____ story   e. the form of literature that consists of poems

6. _____ writing   f. a description of imaginary people and events

7. _____ poetry   g. books and poetry that are considered to be of high quality

8. _____ myth   h. an old story about gods

9. _____ tale   i. something that has been written or printed

10. _____ riddle   j. a story

                 k. a story about a crime

B. Underline the correct word to complete each sentence.

1. Kimberly told us a (**tale / poetry**) about a polar bear trying to survive in Alaska.

2. There is a Greek (**literature / myth**) about a man and his son who want to fly.

3. As Jack read the (**mystery / literature**) he tried to figure out who did the crime.

4. To help us answer the (**riddle / legend**), Sonny gave us several clues.

5. Melinda wrote a (**story / poetry**) about how she learned how to drive a car.

6. As the newspaper's editor, Anne checks the (**writing / myths**) reporters send to her.

7. For many years, there was a (**legend / riddle**) about a monster living deep inside the forest.

8. He writes children's (**mystery / fiction**) and poetry.

9. Shakespeare's plays are considered classic (**literature / riddles**).

10. Many poets have published collections of (**poetry / legends**).

Challenge Words

Check (✔) the words you already know.

☐ comedy   ☐ parable   ☐ proverb   ☐ verse

☐ fable   ☐ prose   ☐ suspense

248. Publication Types

Check (✔) the words you already know. Then, listen and repeat.

Tracks 1–17

☐ **book**
TR 1

☐ **bible**
TR 2

☐ **textbook**
TR 3

☐ **magazine**
TR 6

☐ **booklet**
TR 7

☐ **novel**
TR 8

☐ **essay**
TR 9

☐ **outline**
TR 12

☐ **diary**
☐ **journal**
TR 13 and TR 14

☐ **summary**
TR 16

☐ **dictionary**
TR 15

□ **cookbook**

TR 4

□ **storybook**

TR 5

□ **chapter**

TR 11

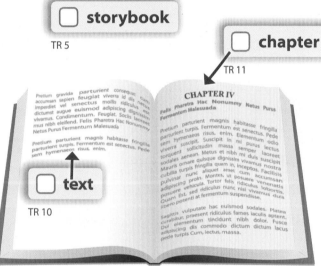

□ **text**

TR 10

□ **newspaper**

TR 17

Definitions

The **bible** is the holy book of the Christian and Jewish religions.

A **book** is a number of pieces of paper, usually with words printed on them, kept together with a paper or hard cover.

A **booklet** is a small book with a few pages that gives you information on one topic.

A **chapter** is a part of a book.

A **cookbook** is a book that tells you how to prepare different meals.

A **diary** is a book that has a separate space for each day of the year. You use a diary to write down things that you plan to do, or to record what happens in your life.

A **dictionary** is a book in which the words and phrases of a language are listed, together with their meanings.

An **essay** is a short piece of writing on a subject.

A **journal** is a notebook or diary.

A **magazine** is a thin book with stories and pictures that you can buy every week or every month.

A **newspaper** is a number of large sheets of folded paper, with news, advertisements, and other information printed on them.

A **novel** is a long written story about imaginary people and events.

An **outline** is a general explanation or description of something.

A **storybook** is a book of stories for children.

A **summary** is a short description that gives the main points of a topic but not the details.

Text is all the words that make up a book, a document, a newspaper, or a magazine.

A **textbook** is a book containing facts about a particular subject that is used by people studying that subject.

Check Your Understanding

A. Circle the response that correctly completes each sentence.

1. I use a **cookbook** to _____ .

   a. fix my bike's flat tire

   b. bake a cake

   c. buy a movie ticket

2. I read a **novel** to _____ .

   a. exercise

   b. watch a TV show

   c. imagine how characters live

3. I read a **newspaper** to _____ .

   a. learn about daily events

   b. sing my favorite songs

   c. send messages to my friends

4. I create an **outline** to _____ .

   a. paint a picture

   b. write a summary

   c. play tennis

5. One type of **book** is a _____ .

   a. cookie

   b. novel

   c. fast car

6. A **storybook** includes many _____ .

   a. titles and lists

   b. planets and moons

   c. stories and pictures

7. I read a fashion **magazine** to _____ .

   a. see the latest clothing styles

   b. do my math homework

   c. join a club

8. I write a **summary** to _____ .

   a. look up a word

   b. take out the trash

   c. state the main ideas

9. The **bible** is the holy book for _____ religions.

   a. Christian and Buddhist

   b. Christian and Jewish

   c. Islamic and Jewish

10. Charlotte couldn't understand the **text** because _____ .

    a. she was thirsty

    b. she forgot her keys

    c. it was written in another language

11. The novel is divided into **chapters**, which _____ a book.

    a. organize

    b. read

    c. spell

12. A **textbook** is used by _____ .

    a. bankers to count money

    b. students in school

    c. cooks in restaurants

13. Most **booklets** contain _____ .

    a. songs about heroes and kings

    b. key facts about specific topics

    c. prices of train tickets

14. I use a **journal** to _____ .

    a. record what I did each day   b. predict the weather   c. paint a picture

15. I use a **dictionary** to _____ .

    a. find roads on maps   b. do my math homework   c. look up meanings of words

16. A **diary** is similar to a _____ .

    a. journal   b. dictionary   c. cookbook

17. When I write an **essay**, I usually _____ .

    a. paint a picture   b. perform a play   c. write what I think

B. Circle the word that does not belong in each group.

1. outline	textbook	cookbook
2. newspaper	magazine	summary
3. diary	novel	journal
4. book	essay	storybook
5. summary	outline	textbook
6. booklet	textbook	novel
7. diary	journal	chapter
8. book	magazine	bible
9. text	cookbook	book
10. dictionary	summary	outline
11. essay	book	newspaper
12. newspaper	booklet	storybook
13. bible	outline	essay
14. chapter	newspaper	novel
15. novel	textbook	diary
16. cookbook	newspaper	magazine
17. textbook	journal	book

Challenge Words

Check (✔) the words you already know.

☐ almanac   ☐ atlas   ☐ bibliography   ☐ document   ☐ thesaurus

☐ article   ☐ autobiography   ☐ biography   ☐ glossary   ☐ thesis

256. Messages

Check (✔) the words you already know. Then, listen and repeat.

Tracks 1–7

☐ **valentine**

TR 1

☐ **note**

TR 2

☐ **signal**

TR 3

YIELD TO PEDESTRIANS

☐ **postcard**

TR 4

Definitions

A **letter** is a written message usually sent by mail.

A **message** is a piece of information that you send to or leave for someone.

A **note** is a short, written message.

A **postcard** is a thin card, often with a picture on one side, that you can write on and mail to someone.

A **poster** is a large notice or picture that you stick on a wall.

A **signal** is an action, sound, or sign that sends a particular message to someone, often without using words.

A **valentine** or a valentine card is a letter or card given to a person to show affection or love on Saint Valentine's Day, February 14.

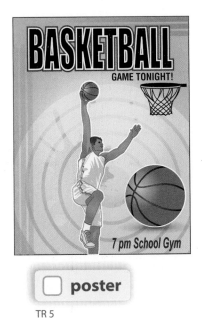

☐ **poster**

TR 5

☐ **letter**

TR 6

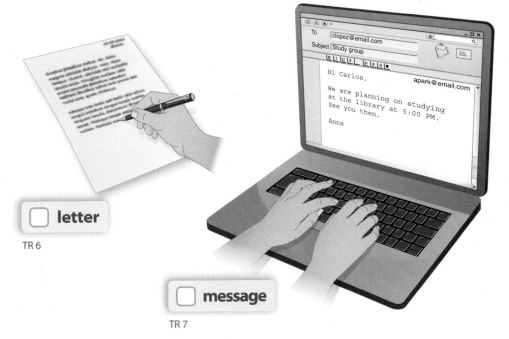

☐ **message**

TR 7

Check Your Understanding

A. Underline the correct word to complete each sentence.

1. Caroline made her mother a beautiful (**signal** / **valentine**) decorated with hearts.

2. During her trip to New York City, Victor's aunt mailed him a (**message** / **postcard**) with a picture of the Statue of Liberty.

3. Barbara wrote a thank-you (**letter** / **signal**) to her grandfather.

4. Charlie left a (**note** / **poster**) for his mother on the kitchen table to let her know that he had gone to the store.

5. The man waved a light as a (**signal** / **valentine**) for the plane to land.

6. The school cafeteria is decorated with (**letters** / **posters**) for the basketball game this Friday.

7. I sent a (**message** / **postcard**) to Cecilia to tell her that I would be late for our meeting.

B. Circle the word that matches the meaning of each **boldfaced** word or phrase.

1. The **information he left** was simple: call him back as soon as possible.

   a. message   b. letter   c. postcard

2. To advertise the concert, they hung **large, printed papers with a picture** all over the city.

   a. notes   b. posters   c. letters

3. Simon gave a **decorated card** to his sister on Valentine's Day.

   a. valentine   b. message   c. note

4. I received a **card with a picture on the front** from my uncle who is traveling in Singapore.

   a. note   b. postcard   c. letter

5. Teddy received a **message written on paper** from the company that is offering him a job.

   a. poster   b. valentine   c. letter

6. The teacher gave a **nod** to tell the students to quiet down.

   a. poster   b. note   c. signal

7. Peter read the **short, informal letter** from his mother.

   a. note   b. postcard   c. valentine

Challenge Words

Check (✔) the words you already know.

☐ advertisement   ☐ commercial   ☐ motto

☐ billboard   ☐ memo   ☐ slogan

279. Illustrations and Drawings

Check (✔) the words you already know. Then, listen and repeat.

 Tracks 1–4

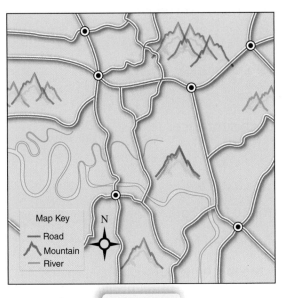

☐ **map**

TR 1

Definitions

A **diagram** is a drawing with markings to show how something works or how it is put together.

A **drawing** is a picture made with a pencil or pen.

A **graph** is a picture that shows the relationship between sets of numbers or measurements.

A **map** is a representation of a geographic location that shows things like mountains, rivers, and roads.

☐ **diagram**

TR 2

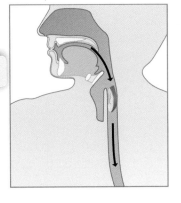

☐ **drawing**

TR 4

☐ **graph**

TR 3

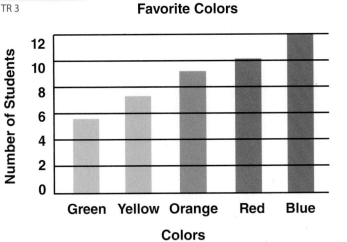

Favorite Colors

Check Your Understanding

A. Match each word to the correct description. One description will not be used.

1. _____ diagram
2. _____ drawing
3. _____ graph
4. _____ map

a. a picture made with a pencil or pen

b. a representation of a particular area, such as a city

c. a picture that shows how sets of numbers are related

d. a picture made with paint

e. a drawing that shows how something works

B. Choose the best word from the word bank to complete each sentence.

graph	diagram	drawing	map

1. My dad needed a _____ to plan our car trip to New York.

2. During his art class, Ron made a _____ of a bowl of fruit.

3. David drew a simple _____ to show how the machine worked.

4. The measurements were compared using a _____.

Challenge Words

Check (✔) the word if you already know it.

☐ chart

319. Titles and Names

Check (✔) the words you already know. Then, listen and repeat.

Tracks 1–3

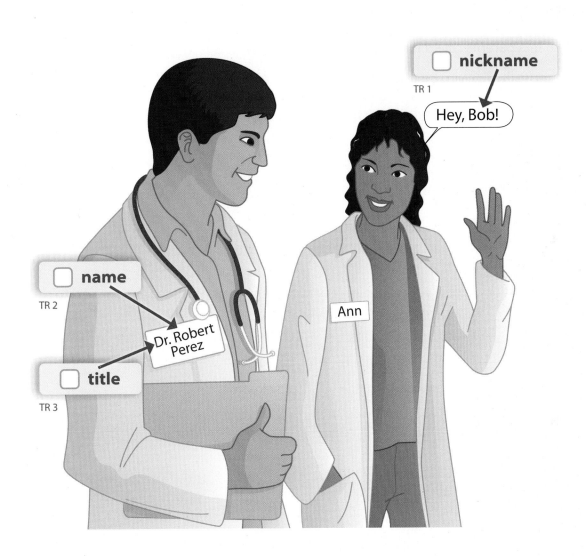

☐ **nickname**

TR 1

Hey, Bob!

☐ **name**

TR 2

Dr. Robert Perez

☐ **title**

TR 3

Ann

Definitions

A person's **name** is the word or words that you use to identify that person.

A **nickname** is an informal name for someone or something.

A **title** is a word or an abbreviation that is used with a person's name to show his or her profession, rank, or marital status.

Check Your Understanding

A. Choose the sentence that correctly uses the underlined word.

1. a. During class, the students used the <u>title</u> *Professor* when asking the teacher questions.

    b. After a swim in the lake, Irene went for a ride on the <u>title</u>.

2. a. Michael's parents called him by his <u>nickname</u>, Mike.

    b. James walked down the driveway to collect the <u>nickname</u>.

3. a. The family traveled to the city to shop for some <u>names</u>.

    b. His <u>name</u> is Frederick, but his friends call him Fred.

B. Circle the word that matches the meaning of each **boldfaced** phrase.

1. My sister is **identified by the word** Shay.

    a. titled   b. named   c. nicknamed

2. After the election, people will call the new president by his or her **name that is used to show rank.**

    a. title   b. name   c. nickname

3. Because she was so small, Tina's friends called her by her **informal name,** Tiny.

    a. title   b. name   c. nickname

Challenge Words

Check (✔) the words you already know.

- ☐ autograph
- ☐ brand
- ☐ identify
- ☐ monogram
- ☐ signature
- ☐ trademark

320. Rules and Laws

Check (✔) the words you already know. Then, listen and repeat.

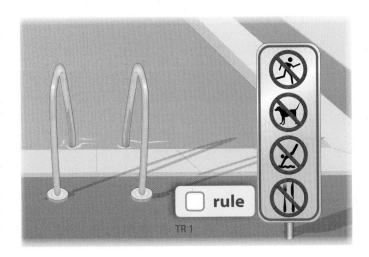

☐ **rule**

TR 1

Definitions

The **law** is a system of rules that a society or a government develops to deal with things like crime.

A **regulation** is a rule that says how something should be done.

A **rule** is an instruction that tells you what you must do or must not do.

☐ **law**

TR 2

☐ **regulation**

TR 3

CONSTRUCTION ZONE

Check Your Understanding

A. Choose the best word from the word bank to complete each sentence.

laws	rules	regulations

1. There are many _____ about food and drug safety in the United States.
2. The government develops the _____ of our country.
3. Eric understands the _____ of the game of chess.

B. Choose the sentence that correctly uses the underlined word.

1. a. Benjamin took the <u>rule</u> and put it in his backpack.

   b. One of the <u>rules</u> of this school is that students may not eat during class.

2. a. We used a <u>law</u> to cut the paper in half.

   b. The government passed a new <u>law</u> against air pollution.

3. a. According to the soccer team <u>regulations</u>, all players must wear red and white uniforms.

   b. At the end of the movie, the <u>regulations</u> appeared on the screen.

Challenge Words

Check (✔) the words you already know.

☐ charter   ☐ contract   ☐ diploma   ☐ treaty

☐ constitution   ☐ curfew   ☐ policy

54. Music and Dance

Check (✔) the words you already know. Then, listen and repeat.

Tracks 1–6

☐ **music**

TR 1

Definitions

Ballet is a type of dancing with formal movements, usually to classical music.

A **dance** is a particular series of movements that you usually do in time to music.

A **melody** is a tune or a song.

Music is the art of putting sounds into a pleasant sequence.

An **orchestra** is a large group of musicians who play different instruments together.

A **solo** is a piece of music or a dance that is written for and performed by only one person or one instrument.

☐ **solo**

TR 2

☐ **melody**

TR 3

☐ **dance**

TR 4

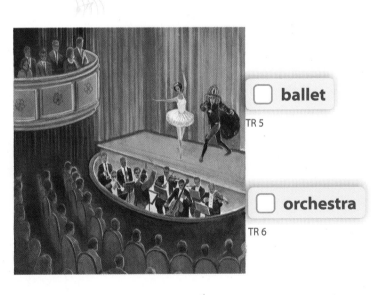

☐ **ballet**

TR 5

☐ **orchestra**

TR 6

99

Check Your Understanding

A. Choose the correct word from the word bank to complete each sentence. One word will not be used.

dance	ballet	melody	solo
pantomime	music	orchestra	

1. The other singers were silent as Peter began to sing his _____ .

2. Terry and Vivian often went to the _____ because they liked the classical music and beautiful dancing.

3. There are many different musical instruments in an _____ .

4. Cindy played a short _____ on the trumpet.

5. Tango, ballet, waltz, and hip-hop are types of _____ .

6. Laura likes to listen to _____ on the radio.

B. Underline the correct word to complete each sentence.

1. (**Orchestra / Ballet**) is a very difficult type of dance to learn.

2. Salsa is a type of (**melody / dance**) that Roberto and Nora practice.

3. The members of the (**orchestra / music**) sat on the stage, ready to perform.

4. Anna sang a (**ballet / solo**) during the concert.

5. Nathan turned on his MP3 player to listen to the (**music / dance**).

6. Brianne played a happy (**melody / ballet**) on the piano.

Challenge Words

Check (✔) the words you already know.

☐ concert ☐ jazz ☐ opera ☐ tune

☐ duet ☐ musical ☐ pantomime ☐ waltz

77. Movies and Plays

Check (✔) the words you already know. Then, listen and repeat.

Tracks 1–8

☐ **cartoon**

TR 1

☐ **comedy**

TR 2

Definitions

If you **act** in a play, movie, or television program, you have a part in it.

A **cartoon** is a film that uses drawings for all the characters and scenes instead of real people or objects.

A **comedy** is a play, a movie, or a television program that tries to make people laugh.

A **film** is a movie.

A **movie** is a story that is shown in a series of moving pictures.

A **play** is a piece of writing performed in a theater, on the radio, or on television.

A **show** is a play, movie, television program, or other entertainment that people watch.

In a theater, the **stage** is the area where people perform.

☐ **film**
☐ **movie**

TR 3 and TR 4

☐ **act**

TR 5

☐ **play**

TR 6

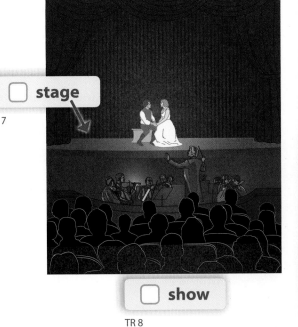

☐ **stage**

TR 7

☐ **show**

TR 8

Check Your Understanding

A. Underline the correct word to complete each sentence.

1. Tyler's favorite (**act / cartoon**) is *Speed Racer*.

2. The actors stood near the edge of the (**film / stage**) to take a bow.

3. A (**movie / play**) tells a story through moving pictures.

4. Another word for *movie* is (**comedy / film**).

5. Raymond left the theater when the (**show / stage**) ended.

6. Cynthia will (**film / act**) in the school play.

7. Jeff wrote a short (**play / movie**) for his class to perform at the school talent show.

8. Mary and Sue laughed out loud while they watched the (**act / comedy**) show.

B. Choose the sentence that correctly uses the underlined word.

1. a. Nancy planned to take her children to see a <u>show</u>.

   b. The actors walked onto the <u>show</u> and bowed.

2. a. A <u>play</u> is used when you hang a picture.

   b. Andy went to the theater to see a <u>play</u>.

3. a. Domenic and Jacob bought chips and sodas at the <u>stage</u>.

   b. During the rock concert, the musician jumped off the <u>stage</u>.

4. a. In the theater, you are supposed to be quiet during the <u>movie</u>.

   b. She told me to put the <u>movie</u> in the refrigerator.

5. a. We thought that the new <u>comedy</u> was the funniest show on television.

   b. The violinist began to play a beautiful <u>comedy</u>.

6. a. Marissa rode the <u>film</u> until she reached downtown.

   b. I had a couple of hours of free time, so I watched a <u>film</u>.

7. a. Did you take theater classes to learn how to <u>act</u>?

   b. Lucas got up, <u>acted</u>, and ate breakfast before leaving for school.

8. a. During the morning, that television channel shows only <u>cartoons</u>.

   b. My father brought the <u>cartoon</u> to the mechanic to get it fixed.

Challenge Words

Check (✔) the words you already know.

- [ ] drama
- [ ] perform
- [ ] plot
- [ ] rehearsal
- [ ] scene
- [ ] setting

239. Art

Check (✔) the words you already know. Then, listen and repeat.

 Tracks 1–6

☐ **photo**
☐ **photograph**

TR 1 and TR 2

Definitions

Art is pictures or objects that are created to express beauty. Painting, sculpture, music, literature, and dance are some different types of art.

A **painting** is a work of art that someone has painted.

A **photo** is the same as a photograph.

A **photograph** is a picture taken with a camera.

A **picture** is a drawing, photograph, or painting.

A **statue** is the form of a person or an animal, usually made of stone or metal.

☐ **art**

TR 3

☐ **picture**

TR 4

☐ **statue**

TR 6

☐ **painting**

TR 5

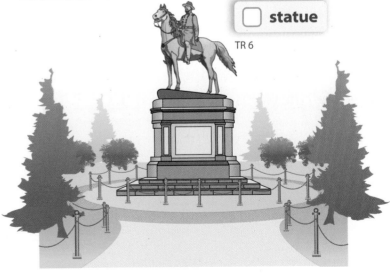

Check Your Understanding

A. Underline the correct word to complete each sentence.

1. Eli drew a (**art / picture**) of his pet dog.

2. We admired the (**painting / statue**) that was hanging on the wall.

3. Sandy took a (**photo / art**) of her mom and dad.

4. The (**photograph / statue**) of Abraham Lincoln at the Lincoln Memorial is made of marble.

5. Our class visited the museum to look at the collection of modern (**art / picture**).

6. Another word for (**painting / photograph**) is *photo*.

B. Circle the word that could replace the underlined word or phrase in the sentence without changing its meaning.

1. The large model of George Washington was made of shiny metal.

    a. statue   b. painting   c. photo

2. Henry took the picture with his camera.

    a. statue   b. photo   c. art

3. The collection of pictures and objects in the museum was displayed for everyone to see.

    a. art   b. statue   c. picture

4. Pointing her camera at the sunset, Susan took a photo.

    a. photograph   b. painting   c. statue

5. A painted image that my son made hangs on the refrigerator door.

    a. photo   b. painting   c. statue

6. To draw an image of his family, David used colorful markers.

    a. an art   b. a statue   c. a picture

Challenge Words

Check (✔) the words you already know.

☐ album   ☐ mural   ☐ portrait

☐ mosaic   ☐ portfolio   ☐ snapshot

244. Musical Instruments

Check (✔) the words you already know. Then, listen and repeat.

 Tracks 1–7

☐ **banjo**
TR 1

☐ **drum**
TR 2

☐ **guitar**
TR 3

Definitions

A **banjo** is a musical instrument that looks like a guitar with a round body, a long neck, and four or more strings.

A **drum** is a simple musical instrument that you hit with sticks or with your hands.

A **guitar** is a musical instrument with strings that you play with your fingers or with a pick.

A musical **instrument** is an object that you use for making music.

A **piano** is a large musical instrument that you play by pressing black and white keys.

A **triangle** is a small, metal musical instrument in the shape of a triangle. You play it by hitting it with a small, metal bar.

A **violin** is a musical instrument made of wood with four strings. You hold it under your chin and play it by moving a long stick called a bow across the strings.

☐ **piano**
TR 4

☐ **triangle**
TR 5

☐ **violin**
TR 6

☐ **instrument**
TR 7

Check Your Understanding

A. Match each word to the correct description. One description will not be used.

1. _____ guitar
2. _____ piano
3. _____ instrument
4. _____ violin
5. _____ triangle
6. _____ banjo
7. _____ drum

a. an instrument you play by blowing

b. an object you use for making music

c. an instrument made of metal that you hit with a small, metal bar

d. an instrument that you play using a bow

e. an instrument that looks like a guitar

f. an instrument that you play using sticks

g. a large instrument with black and white keys

h. a musical instrument with strings

B. Write **T** for **true statements** and **F** for **false statements**.

1. _____ You play a piano by pressing on its black and white strings.

2. _____ An instrument is used for making music.

3. _____ A triangle is an instrument made of metal.

4. _____ Guitars have many keys that you press to make music.

5. _____ A banjo has six or more strings.

6. _____ You play a drum by hitting it with a bow or your hands.

7. _____ You hold a violin under your chin as you play it.

Challenge Words

Check (✔) the words you already know.

☐ cello

☐ clarinet

☐ flute

☐ harmonica

☐ keyboard

☐ saxophone

☐ trumpet

☐ ukulele

135. Looking and Perceiving

Check (✔) the words you already know. Then, listen and repeat.

Tracks 1–8

☐ **look**
TR 1

☐ **see**
TR 2

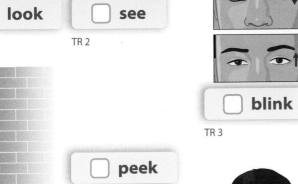

☐ **blink**
TR 3

☐ **peek**
TR 4

☐ **wink**
TR 5

☐ **spy**
TR 6

Definitions

When you **blink**, you shut your eyes and very quickly open them again.

If you **look** in a particular direction, you turn your eyes so that you can see what is there.

If you **peek**, you look at something or someone quickly when you are not supposed to.

When you **see** something, you notice it using your eyes.

If you **spy**, you watch someone or something secretly.

When you **stare**, you look at someone or something steadily and with your eyes wide-open.

When you **watch** someone or something, you look at that person or thing for a period of time.

When you **wink**, you close and open one eye quickly, usually as a sign that something is a joke or a secret.

☐ **watch**
TR 7

☐ **stare**
TR 8

Check Your Understanding

A. Underline the correct word to complete each sentence.

1. My family likes to (**watch / blink**) soccer games at the park.

2. Before I entered the dark hallway, I quickly (**peeked / stared**) around the corner.

3. Everyone (**winked / stared**) when the new student walked into the room.

4. Mary (**looked / blinked**) for her mother in the crowd of people.

5. Walking out of the dark movie theater and into the bright sunlight made me (**watch / blink**).

6. Hannah asked her brother if she could (**spy / see**) his new camera.

7. My grandfather always (**winks / watches**) when he makes jokes.

8. Andrew looked through the door and (**spied / winked**) Susan wrapping his birthday gift.

B. Choose the sentence that correctly uses the underlined word.

1. a. I <u>looked</u> all over my room to find my favorite book.

   b. Justin closed his eyes so that he could <u>look</u> out the window.

2. a. My father closed one eye to <u>see</u> at me.

   b. We will <u>see</u> elephants, tigers, and clowns at the circus.

3. a. Dave quickly <u>stared</u> at the waterfall and kept walking.

   b. We <u>stared</u> straight ahead at the traffic signal, waiting for the light to change.

4. a. I like to <u>watch</u> airplanes and helicopters flying in the sky.

   b. I wanted to <u>watch</u> my favorite color today.

5. a. When the coach trained the team, he <u>blinked</u> them to run a mile.

   b. Every time the camera light flashed, I <u>blinked</u> my eyes.

6. a. Josie is only two years old, so she doesn't know how to <u>peek</u> her shoes by herself.

   b. Erik and his sister <u>peeked</u> into the box to see what was inside.

7. a. It is important to <u>spy</u> your food before you finish eating.

   b. Kendra tried to <u>spy</u> the neighbor's cat through the cracks in the fence.

8. a. When I <u>winked</u>, my best friend knew that our secret was safe.

   b. Robert <u>winked</u> the windows and doors in his house every day.

Challenge Words

Check (✔) the words you already know.

- [ ] detect
- [ ] gaze
- [ ] ignore
- [ ] perceive
- [ ] focus
- [ ] identify
- [ ] observe
- [ ] recognize

195. Visual Perceptions and Images

Check (✔) the words you already know. Then, listen and repeat.

Tracks 1–7

☐ **appearance**
TR 1

☐ **badge**
TR 2

Definitions

A person's or thing's **appearance** is the way that person or thing looks.

A **badge** is a small piece of metal or plastic that you wear on your clothes to show people who you are.

A **flag** is a piece of colored cloth with a pattern on it that is used as a symbol for a country or an organization.

An **image** is a mental picture of someone or something in your mind.

The **scene** of an event is the place where it happened.

Sight is the physical sense of seeing.

The **view** from a location is all of the things that can be seen from that location.

☐ **flag**
TR 3

☐ **image**
TR 4

☐ **scene**
TR 5

☐ **sight**
TR 6

☐ **view**
TR 7

Check Your Understanding

A. Choose the correct word from the word bank to complete each sentence. One word will not be used.

badge	view	sight	flag
witness	scene	image	appearance

1. The ambulance raced to the _____ of the accident.

2. The security officer's _____ , which he wore on his shirt, showed his first and last name.

3. The _____ of people screaming while riding the roller coaster frightened Tina.

4. When Carol finally got a job in a large company, it was very different from the _____ she had held in her mind for so many years.

5. From the top of the building, the _____ of the city was incredible.

6. Everyone noticed the change in Heidi's _____ : she looked thin, her hair was a different color, and she was wearing all black clothing.

7. Our state _____ hangs in the capitol building.

B. Circle the word that could replace the underlined word or phrase in the sentence without changing its meaning.

1. My mother wears glasses to improve her <u>sense of seeing</u>.
   a. flag   b. badge   c. sight

2. Carl was afraid of the neighbor's dog because of its mean and angry <u>look</u>.
   a. appearance   b. flag   c. sight

3. The soldier saluted the <u>piece of cloth that symbolizes a country</u> that was hanging from the pole.
   a. image   b. flag   c. scene

4. When the woman tried on her wedding dress, it was the same as the <u>picture</u> she had in her mind.
   a. sight   b. image   c. flag

5. Main Street is the <u>place</u> where the bank robbery happened.
   a. scene   b. appearance   c. view

6. The police officer showed us his <u>small piece of metal to identify him</u>.
   a. flag   b. badge   c. view

7. Meghan had a good seat. Nobody was blocking the <u>things that could be seen</u> of the stage.
   a. flag   b. image   c. view

Challenge Words

Check (✔) the words you already know.

☐ demonstration   ☐ identify   ☐ reflect   ☐ scope

☐ display   ☐ phenomenon   ☐ reveal   ☐ witness

47. Things Worn on the Head

Check (✔) the words you already know. Then, listen and repeat.

Tracks 1–8

☐ mask
TR 1

☐ hood
TR 2

☐ crown
TR 3

Definitions

A **cap** is a soft hat with a curved part at the front.

A **crown** is a decoration made of gold and jewels that is worn on someone's head. A crown is usually worn by a king or queen.

Glasses are two lenses in a frame that some people wear to help them to see better.

A **hat** is an item of clothing that you wear on your head.

A **helmet** is a hat made of a hard material worn to protect your head.

A **hood** is the part of a coat that you can pull up to cover your head.

A **mask** is something that you wear over your face to protect it or to hide it.

Sunglasses are colored lenses that you wear to protect your eyes from bright light such as the sun.

☐ hat
TR 4

☐ glasses
TR 5

☐ sunglasses
TR 6

☐ helmet
TR 7

☐ cap
TR 8

Check Your Understanding

A. Match each word to the correct description. One description will not be used.

1. _____ hat
2. _____ helmet
3. _____ mask
4. _____ crown
5. _____ sunglasses
6. _____ hood
7. _____ glasses
8. _____ cap

a. a soft hat with a curved part at the front

b. a pair of lenses in a frame that people wear to help them see

c. a thing that you wear on your head

d. a hat made of a hard material

e. a piece of thin, soft cloth that women sometimes wear over their heads on their wedding day

f. something that you wear to cover your face

g. dark glasses

h. a gold decoration that a queen wears on her head

i. the part of a coat that you can pull up to cover your head

B. Choose the correct word from the word bank to complete each sentence. One word will not be used.

visor	hat	cap
hood	helmet	masks
glasses	sunglasses	crown

1. Emily put on her _____ to protect her eyes from the bright sun.

2. When he played football, Tony always wore his _____ to protect his head.

3. It was so cold, Barbara pulled up her _____ to cover her head.

4. When Henry joined the baseball team, he received a uniform and a soft, red, baseball _____ .

5. Susan needs her _____ to help her read the small letters.

6. The king wore a golden _____ that sparkled with jewels.

7. The criminals wore _____ to hide their faces completely.

8. My grandmother's favorite _____ is made of straw and decorated with a ribbon and flowers.

Challenge Words

Check (✔) the words you already know.

- [ ] beret
- [ ] bonnet
- [ ] goggles
- [ ] headdress
- [ ] spectacles
- [ ] tiara
- [ ] turban
- [ ] veil
- [ ] visor

62. Things Worn on the Hands / Feet

Check (✔) the words you already know. Then, listen and repeat.

 Tracks 1–9

☐ **boot**
TR 1

☐ **glove**
TR 2

☐ **mittens**
TR 3

☐ **shoe**
TR 4

☐ **skate**
TR 5

☐ **sock**
TR 6

Definitions

A **boot** is a shoe that covers your whole foot and the lower part of your leg.

A **glove** is a piece of clothing that you wear on your hand, with a separate part for each finger.

Mittens are gloves that have one part that covers your thumb and another part that covers your four fingers together.

A **shoe** is a covering that you wear on your foot and often has a sole and a heel.

A **skate** is a boot that has wheels on the bottom of it so that you can move quickly on the ground. Another type of skate has a blade on the bottom and is used to move quickly over ice.

A **sock** is a piece of clothing that covers your foot and ankle.

A **stocking** is a piece of women's clothing that fits closely over the foot and leg.

A **sandal** is a light shoe that you wear in warm weather.

A **slipper** is a loose, soft shoe that you wear indoors.

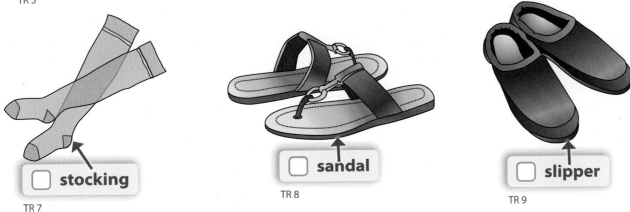

☐ **stocking**
TR 7

☐ **sandal**
TR 8

☐ **slipper**
TR 9

113

Check Your Understanding

A. Match each word to the correct description. One description will not be used.

1. _____ sandal
2. _____ mittens
3. _____ glove
4. _____ shoe
5. _____ slipper
6. _____ boot
7. _____ stocking
8. _____ sock
9. _____ skate

a. a soft shoe that you wear indoors

b. a light shoe that you wear outdoors

c. a piece of women's clothing that fits closely over the feet and legs

d. a piece of clothing that you wear on your feet and with shoes

e. a boot that has wheels

f. special type of heavy glove worn by baseball players

g. gloves that have one part that covers your thumb and another part that covers your four fingers

h. a piece of clothing that you wear on your hands

i. a shoe that covers your whole foot and the lower part of your leg

j. a covering that you wear on your feet that has a sole and a heel

B. Write the words from the word bank in the correct column.

boot	sandal	sock
glove	mittens	shoe
slipper	stocking	skate

CLOTHING WORN ON THE HANDS	CLOTHING WORN ON THE FEET

Challenge Words

Check (✔) the words you already know.

☐ garter ☐ mitt ☐ moccasin

125. Pants, Shirts, and Skirts

Check (✔) the words you already know. Then, listen and repeat.

Tracks 1–16

⬜ **pajamas**

TR 1

⬜ **bathrobe**

TR 2

⬜ **jeans**

TR 3

⬜ **sweater**

TR 4

⬜ **shirt**

TR 5

⬜ **dress**

TR 6

⬜ **shorts**

TR 7

⬜ **pocket**

TR 8

⬜ **pants**

TR 9

⬜ **diaper**

TR 10

115

☐ **apron**

TR 11

☐ **nightgown**

TR 12

☐ **robe**

TR 13

☐ **belt**

TR 14

☐ **tights**

TR 15

☐ **skirt**

TR 16

Definitions

An **apron** is a covering worn over the front of your body, in order to prevent your clothes from getting dirty, especially when cooking.

A **bathrobe** is a long, loose piece of clothing that you wear at home after taking a bath or shower.

A **belt** is a strip of leather or cloth that you wear around your waist to hold up your pants or as decoration.

A **diaper** is a piece of soft, thick cloth or paper covered in plastic that you fasten around a baby's bottom and between its legs.

A **dress** is a piece of clothing for women and girls that covers the top part of the body and part of the legs.

Jeans are pants that are made of strong cotton cloth, called *denim*.

A **nightgown** is a loose dress that a woman or a girl wears for sleeping.

Pajamas are loose pants and a top that people wear for sleeping.

Pants are a piece of clothing worn by men and women, which run from the waist to the ankles with two long sections for the legs.

A **pocket** is a small bag sewn into clothes that is used for holding things.

A **robe** is a long piece of clothing that you wear in the house before you get dressed.

A **shirt** is a piece of clothing with sleeves, a collar, and buttons that you wear on the top part of your body.

Shorts are pants that end at or above the knee.

A **skirt** is a piece of clothing for women and girls that hangs down from the waist and covers part of the legs.

A **sweater** is a warm piece of clothing that covers the upper part of your body and your arms.

Tights are a piece of close-fitting clothing that covers the lower body and legs. Tights are worn by women, girls, and dancers.

Check Your Understanding

A. Write the words from the word bank in the correct column.

shirt	tights	skirt	belt
dress	pocket	jeans	robe
pants	pajamas	apron	shorts
bathrobe	nightgown	sweater	diaper

CLOTHING WORN ON THE UPPER BODY	CLOTHING WORN ON THE LOWER BODY	CLOTHING THAT COVERS THE WHOLE BODY	ACCESSORIES AND PARTS OF CLOTHING

B. Underline the correct word to complete each sentence.

1. The (**shorts / tights**) kept the dancers' legs warm.

2. Before going outside to play, Lisa put on her (**nightgown / sweater**).

3. The cook wore the (**robe / apron**) to keep his clothes clean.

4. After her shower, Gloria put on a (**tights / bathrobe**).

5. The man watched television dressed in his pajamas and (**robe / shorts**).

6. It was a hot day, so most people wore (**shorts / sweaters**) at the beach.

7. Lucy put on her (**nightgown / belt**) and climbed into bed for a good night's rest.

8. At Michelle's school, the girls have to wear white shirts and dark blue (**pajamas / skirts**) to class.

9. The (**jeans / belts**) were made of black leather and had a silver buckle.

10. His white (**diaper / shirt**) has three buttons and a wide collar.

11. Stella bought a special (**robe / dress**) to wear to the elegant party.

12. Most children stop wearing (**diapers / pockets**) by the time they are three years old.

13. Joe put his keys in his (**pocket / belt**) so that they wouldn't get lost.

14. Most students, boys and girls alike, wear (**tights / jeans**) to school every day.

15. Martin put on his (**pajamas / nightgown**) before he went to sleep.

16. Jack put on his shirt and (**pants / robe**) before leaving the house.

Challenge Words

Check (✔) the words you already know.

☐ blouse	☐ gown	☐ kimono	☐ petticoat	☐ slacks
☐ cardigan	☐ jersey	☐ overalls	☐ pullover	☐ vest

129. Clothing-Related Actions

Check (✔) the words you already know. Then, listen and repeat.

Tracks 1–10

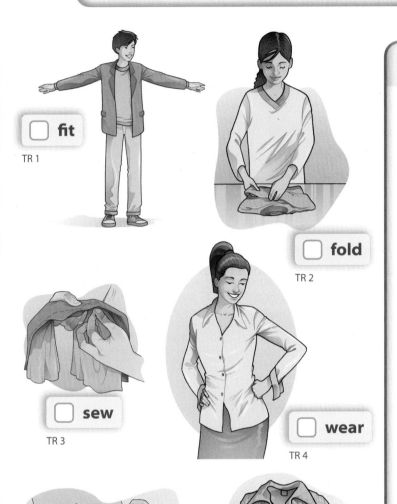

☐ **fit**

TR 1

☐ **fold**

TR 2

☐ **sew**

TR 3

☐ **wear**

TR 4

Definitions

To **braid** means to put pieces of fabric or hair around and between each other.

To **fit** means a piece of clothing is the right size for someone or something.

To **fold** a cloth means to turn one part of it over another part.

To **patch** means to use a piece of cloth to cover a hole in a piece of clothing.

To **rip** means to tear something apart.

To **sew** means to join pieces of cloth together using a needle and thread.

To **tear** means to pull something into pieces or make a hole in it.

When you **wear** clothes, shoes, or jewelry, you have them on your body.

To **wrinkle** means a piece of cloth has folds or lines in it.

To **zip** means to fasten a piece of clothing by using its zipper.

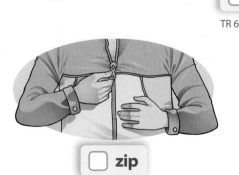

☐ **patch**

TR 5

☐ **wrinkle**

TR 6

☐ **zip**

TR 7

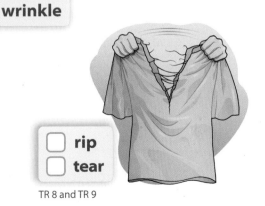

☐ **rip**
☐ **tear**

TR 8 and TR 9

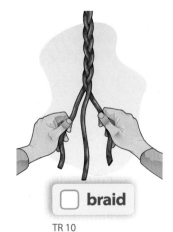

☐ **braid**

TR 10

Check Your Understanding

A. Write **T** for **true statements** and **F** for **false statements**.

1. _____ When you wear clothing, you pull it into pieces.
2. _____ People usually fasten their jackets by braiding them.
3. _____ If you tear a piece of clothing, you make a hole in it.
4. _____ In order to sew clothes, you need glue and stamps.
5. _____ When clothing wrinkles, it gets folds or lines in it.
6. _____ When you fold clothes, you try to crumple them into a ball.
7. _____ If you zip your pants, you fasten them.
8. _____ If you patch clothing, you fix the holes in it.
9. _____ If a shirt doesn't fit someone, it is probably the wrong size.
10. _____ When you rip clothing, it makes a lot of folds in it.

B. Choose the sentence that correctly uses the underlined word.

1. a. Before she went out, the girl asked her friend to braid her hair so it would look nice.
   b. Andrea decided to braid her jeans because there was a hole in them.
2. a. Henry's jeans ripped when they got caught on a nail.
   b. Alexandra neatly ripped her laundry and put it in her dresser.
3. a. Everyone wrinkled when George told the joke.
   b. Paula's dress wrinkled when she sat in the car.
4. a. Pete patched the hole in his jeans.
   b. It was time to patch the table, so we got out the plates and forks.
5. a. I want to buy these pants, but I have to make sure that they fit me.
   b. The sound of a piano playing fit over the sidewalk.
6. a. I folded the glasses and plates and put them away.
   b. Stan likes to fold his shirts before putting them in his suitcase.
7. a. What book do you want to wear?
   b. Which dress do you plan to wear to the wedding?
8. a. Please tear up those rags before you throw them in the trash.
   b. The pens weren't working, so Allie decided to tear them up.
9. a. The waiter needed to sew the meal together before serving it.
   b. Susan liked to sew dresses for her daughter's dolls.
10. a. Liam helped the boy zip his jacket.
    b. I always zip the lights when I leave the house.

Challenge Words

Check (✔) the words you already know.

☐ alter   ☐ crease   ☐ embroider   ☐ rumple   ☐ tatter

☐ clad   ☐ don   ☐ knit   ☐ stitch   ☐ weave

145. Coats

Check (✔) the words you already know. Then, listen and repeat.

Tracks 1–4

☐ **jacket**

TR 1

Definitions

A **cape** is a long coat without sleeves that covers your body and arms.

A **coat** is a piece of clothing with long sleeves that you wear over other clothes when you go outside.

A **jacket** is a short coat with long sleeves.

A **raincoat** is a coat that you can wear to keep dry when it rains.

☐ **cape**

TR 2

☐ **coat**

TR 3

☐ **raincoat**

TR 4

Check Your Understanding

A. Write **T** for **true statements** and **F** for **false statements**.

1. _____ Raincoats are good to wear when it rains.

2. _____ A cape has short sleeves.

3. _____ A jacket covers your legs.

4. _____ You wear a coat over your other clothes.

B. Circle the word that matches the meaning of each bold phrase.

1. Daisy chose a **short coat with long sleeves** to wear to school.

   a. raincoat   b. cape   c. jacket

2. The children wore **long coats without sleeves** as part of their costumes.

   a. capes   b. jackets   c. coats

3. It was a rainy day, so Laura put on her **coat that keeps her dry**.

   a. coat   b. raincoat   c. cape

4. When I want to go for a walk outside in wintertime, I always put on my warmest **piece of clothing with long sleeves**.

   a. cape   b. coat   c. raincoat

Challenge Words

Check (✔) the words you already know.

☐ cloak   ☐ overcoat   ☐ poncho   ☐ topcoat

☐ mantle   ☐ parka   ☐ shawl

26 CLOTHING

178. Fabrics

Check (✔) the words you already know. Then, listen and repeat.

☐ rag
TR 2

☐ cloth
TR 1

☐ cotton
TR 3

Definitions

Cloth is material that is used for making clothing.

Cotton is cloth or thread that is made from the cotton plant.

Lace is a thin, delicate cloth with a design made with patterns of holes.

Leather is animal skin that is used for making shoes, clothes, bags, and furniture.

Nylon is a strong, artificial cloth.

A **rag** is a piece of old cloth that is no longer in good condition.

Silk is a smooth, shiny cloth that is made from very thin threads.

Thread or a **thread** is a long, very thin piece of cotton, nylon, or silk that you use for sewing.

Wool is a material made from animal hair, such as sheep, and is used for making things such as clothes.

☐ lace
TR 4

☐ thread
TR 5

☐ silk
TR 6

☐ leather
TR 7

☐ nylon
TR 8

☐ wool
TR 9

Check Your Understanding

A. Match each word to the correct description. One description will not be used.

1. _____ wool
2. _____ silk
3. _____ nylon
4. _____ leather
5. _____ lace
6. _____ cotton
7. _____ thread
8. _____ rag
9. _____ cloth

a. material that is used to make clothes
b. a very long, thin piece of cotton that you use for sewing
c. a delicate cloth with a design made with patterns of holes
d. a strong, artificial cloth
e. a material made from animal hair
f. a soft cloth that is thick on one side
g. animal skin used for making shoes, clothes, and bags
h. cloth made from the cotton plant
i. a piece of old cloth
j. a smooth, shiny cloth made of very thin threads

B. Choose the sentence that correctly uses the underlined word.

1. a. The woman put on her <u>silk</u> scarf before going to work.
   b. I never wear <u>silk</u> because the rough fabric makes my skin itch.
2. a. Liliana brushed her hair as she looked in the bathroom <u>nylon</u>.
   b. The backpack is made of <u>nylon</u>, so it is strong and long-lasting.
3. a. The museum had many famous <u>rags</u> hanging in the main gallery.
   b. The painter used a <u>rag</u> to wipe up the paint he spilled on the floor.
4. a. Lisa needed more <u>cloth</u> than she expected in order to finish sewing her new curtains.
   b. We watched as the <u>cloth</u> flowed noisily under the bridge.
5. a. We each ordered an ice cream cone with <u>thread</u> on top.
   b. Mariah chose a strong <u>thread</u> to sew the buttons on the jacket.
6. a. The <u>wool</u> sweater made Eddie's skin itch, but it kept him very warm.
   b. Jillian wanted some shiny cloth to make a dress, so she bought some <u>wool</u>.
7. a. Mel bought a few T-shirts made of soft <u>cotton</u>.
   b. This <u>cotton</u> is expensive because it comes from cows.
8. a. Shoes and bags are often made of <u>leather</u> because it is durable yet soft.
   b. Vicky used soap to wash the <u>leather</u> off her face.
9. a. <u>Lace</u> that comes from sheep is the best kind.
   b. Jen took out a fancy <u>lace</u> tablecloth to use for the family dinner.

Challenge Words

Check (✔) the words you already know.

☐ denim   ☐ flannel   ☐ linen   ☐ terry   ☐ velvet
☐ felt   ☐ khaki   ☐ satin   ☐ textile   ☐ yarn

124

212. Clothing Parts

Check (✔) the words you already know. Then, listen and repeat.

Tracks 1–4

☐ **zipper**

TR 1

Definitions

Buttons are small, hard objects that you push through holes to fasten your clothes.

A **collar** is material around the neck of a shirt or coat.

The **sleeves** of a piece of clothing are the parts that cover your arms.

A **zipper** is a metal or plastic fastener with teeth used to open and close clothing or bags.

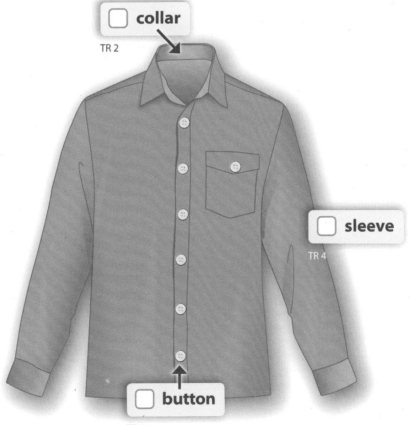

☐ **collar**

TR 2

☐ **sleeve**

TR 4

☐ **button**

TR 3

Check Your Understanding

A. Match each word with the correct description. One description will not be used.

1. _____ button
2. _____ zipper
3. _____ collar
4. _____ sleeve

a. a metal or plastic fastener with teeth

b. the part of a piece of clothing that covers your arms

c. a long, narrow strip of cloth with a lot of folds in it

d. a small, hard object that fastens your clothes

e. the material around the neck of a shirt

B. Write the word from the word bank that correctly completes each sentence. One word will not be used.

collar	cuff	sleeves
zipper	buttons	

1. Karina could not close the front of her jacket because some teeth on the _____ were broken.

2. It was a cool day, so Mimi was glad that she had put on a shirt with long _____.

3. The _____ of Jason's shirt felt tight around his neck, so he chose a larger one.

4. The _____ on Michael's shirt were so small that it was difficult to push them through the holes.

Challenge Words

Check (✔) the words you already know.

☐ bib   ☐ frill   ☐ hem   ☐ ruff   ☐ seam

☐ cuff   ☐ fringe   ☐ pompom   ☐ ruffle   ☐ tassel

224. Clothing and Grooming Accessories

Check (✔) the words you already know. Then, listen and repeat.

☐ jewelry
TR 1

☐ necklace
TR 2

☐ buckle
TR 3

☐ pin
TR 4

☐ comb
TR 5

☐ handkerchief
TR 6

☐ perfume
TR 7

☐ fan
TR 8

☐ brush
TR 9

☐ ribbon
TR 10

☐ kerchief
TR 11

Definitions

A **brush** is an object that has a lot of bristles or hairs attached to it. You use a brush to make your hair neat.

A **comb** is a piece of plastic or metal with teeth. You use a comb to make your hair neat.

A **handkerchief** is a small, square piece of cloth that you use for blowing your nose.

A **buckle** is a piece of metal or plastic on one end of a belt or strap that is used for fastening the belt to your waist.

A **fan** is a flat object that you move backward and forward in front of your face to make you cooler.

Jewelry is a decoration that you wear on your body, such as a ring.

A **kerchief** is a piece of cloth that you wear on your head or around your neck.

A **necklace** is a piece of jewelry that you wear around your neck.

Perfume is a liquid with a pleasant smell that you put on your skin.

A **pin** is a decorative object that you wear on your clothing that is fastened with a pointed piece of metal.

A **ribbon** is a long, narrow piece of cloth that you use to keep things together, or as a decoration.

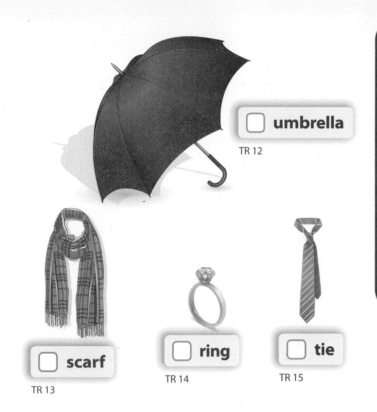

Definitions

A **ring** is a small circle of metal that you wear on your finger.

A **scarf** is a piece of cloth that you wear around your neck or head.

A **tie** or a **necktie** is a long, narrow piece of cloth that you tie in a knot and wear around your neck under the collar of a shirt.

An **umbrella** is a long stick with a cloth or plastic cover that you use to protect yourself from the rain.

☐ umbrella
TR 12

☐ scarf
TR 13

☐ ring
TR 14

☐ tie
TR 15

Check Your Understanding

A. Write **T** for **true statements** and **F** for **false statements**.

1. _____ An umbrella keeps you dry when it's raining.

2. _____ A scarf can be worn around your head.

3. _____ A necklace is used to keep your neck warm.

4. _____ A comb has teeth.

5. _____ On a cold day, you can use a fan to keep you warm.

6. _____ You use a kerchief to wipe your nose.

7. _____ Buckles are usually made of metal.

8. _____ A pin is the metal part of a belt that fastens it.

9. _____ When you wear perfume, you put it on your jewelry.

10. _____ Jewelry is worn for decorative purposes.

11. _____ You wear a handkerchief on your hand.

12. _____ Ribbons are normally worn to decorate your feet.

13. _____ A tie is worn under a shirt.

14. _____ Rings are a kind of jewelry.

15. _____ Brushes are covered in bristles.

B. Circle the word in each group that does *not* belong.

1. umbrella   buckle   strap   belt
2. brush   necklace   hair   bristles
3. square   nose   tie   handkerchief
4. jewelry   pin   ring   kerchief
5. brush   knot   tie   neck
6. rain   protect   umbrella   jewelry
7. skin   smell   perfume   comb
8. fan   tie   necklace   neck
9. kerchief   scarf   tie   ring
10. nose   cloth   pin   handkerchief
11. perfume   ring   finger   metal
12. umbrella   stick   ribbon   cover
13. metal   ring   necklace   handkerchief
14. brush   buckle   hair   comb
15. hair   comb   teeth   scarf

Challenge Words

Check (✔) the words you already know.

☐ bandana   ☐ cane   ☐ cosmetics   ☐ muffler   ☐ razor
☐ bracelet   ☐ cologne   ☐ locket   ☐ pendant   ☐ suspender

263. Clothing (General)

Check (✔) the words you already know. Then, listen and repeat.

Tracks 1–5

☐ **clothes**
☐ **clothing**

TR 1 and TR 2

☐ **costume**

TR 3

Check Your Understanding

A. Match each word to the correct description. One description will use two words.
One word will not be used.

1. _____ special clothes that a person wears to work
2. _____ set of clothes that someone wears in a performance
3. _____ the things that people wear, such as shirts
4. _____ jacket and pants that are made from the same cloth

a. clothes
b. uniform
c. fad
d. clothing
e. suit
f. costume

☐ **suit**

TR 4

☐ **uniform**

TR 5

Definitions

Clothes are the coverings for a person's body, such as shirts, coats, pants, and dresses.

Clothing is what a person wears to cover his or her body.

A **costume** is a set of clothes that someone wears in a performance.

A **suit** consists of a jacket and pants or a skirt that are made from the same cloth.

A **uniform** is the special clothes that some people wear to work and that some children wear in school.

B. Underline the correct word to complete each sentence.

1. The actors put on their (**costumes** / **suits**) and were ready to perform the play.

2. The last step of doing the family's laundry is putting away the (**uniforms** / **clothes**) in each person's room.

3. A shirt is a piece of (**costume** / **clothing**).

4. Before going to work, the police officer made sure that her (**costume** / **uniform**) was clean.

5. Matthew had an important business meeting and decided to wear his black (**suit** / **clothing**).

Challenge Words

Check (✔) the words you already know.

☐ apparel   ☐ design   ☐ fashion   ☐ garment   ☐ style

☐ array   ☐ fad   ☐ garb   ☐ outfit   ☐ wardrobe

354. Characteristics Related to Clothes / Wearing of Clothes

Check (✔) the words you already know. Then, listen and repeat.

 Tracks 1–2

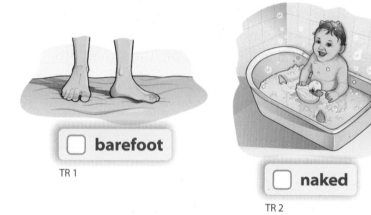

☐ **barefoot**

TR 1

☐ **naked**

TR 2

Definitions

Someone who is **barefoot** is not wearing shoes or socks.

Someone who is **naked** is not wearing any clothes.

Check Your Understanding

A. Choose the sentence that correctly uses the underlined word.

1. a. The baby was <u>naked</u> and dripping wet when he got out of the bathtub.
   b. The <u>naked</u> boy had on a jacket, pants, and a blue shirt.

2. a. After putting on his boots, the <u>barefoot</u> cowboy went for a ride on his horse.
   b. The <u>barefoot</u> girls ran across the grass, which felt soft on their feet.

3. a. The <u>barefoot</u> man bent over to tie his shoelaces.
   b. Carmela helped her <u>barefoot</u> sister put her sandals back on.

B. Write **T** for **true statements** and **F** for **false statements**.

1. _____ People are not normally naked while taking baths or showers.

2. _____ When you are barefoot, you have socks on.

3. _____ If you are barefoot, it's not a good idea to walk outside in the wintertime.

Challenge Words

Check (✔) the words you already know.

☐ bare   ☐ informal   ☐ sheer

☐ bareheaded   ☐ nude   ☐ worn

202. Texture

Check (✔) the words you already know. Then, listen and repeat.

 Tracks 1–7

☐ **bumpy**
TR 1

☐ **soft**
TR 2

☐ **hard**
TR 3

Definitions

Something that is **bumpy** is not smooth or flat.

When something is **firm**, it is solid. It is not soft.

Something that is **hard** feels very firm and is difficult to bend or break.

When a surface is **rough**, it is not smooth or even.

When a surface is **smooth**, it is flat and has no rough parts.

Something that is **soft** is nice to touch and not rough or hard.

When clothes are **tight**, they are small, and they fit closely to your body.

☐ **firm**
TR 4

☐ **tight**
TR 5

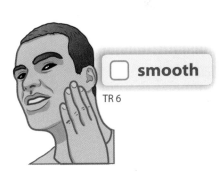

☐ **smooth**
TR 6

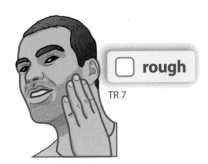

☐ **rough**
TR 7

Check Your Understanding

A. Match each word to the correct description. One description will not be used.

1. _____ rough
2. _____ tight
3. _____ bumpy
4. _____ soft
5. _____ hard
6. _____ firm
7. _____ smooth

a. clothes that are too small and fit closely
b. when a surface is flat and has no bumps or holes
c. something that feels very firm
d. when something is pleasant to touch
e. something that is not smooth or flat
f. when a surface is not smooth or even
g. the way something feels when you touch it
h. when something is not soft

B. Write **T** for **true statements** and **F** for **false statements**.

1. _____ If something is smooth, you can feel very tiny holes in it.
2. _____ Something that is bumpy is always soft.
3. _____ It is difficult to bend or cut a hard object.
4. _____ When something is rough, it feels uneven.
5. _____ If clothes are very tight, they are probably comfortable.
6. _____ It feels nice to touch something that is soft.
7. _____ If something is firm, it feels hard to the touch.

Challenge Words

Check (✔) the words you already know.

☐ coarse   ☐ rigid   ☐ stiff   ☐ taut   ☐ tough

☐ crisp   ☐ solid   ☐ tangible   ☐ texture

323. Durability / Strength

Check (✔) the words you already know. Then, listen and repeat.

Tracks 1–3

☐ **strong**

TR 1

Definitions

Something that is **delicate** can break or become damaged easily.

Strong objects or materials do not break easily and have a lot of physical strength.

Something that is **weak** is not strong and has very little physical strength.

☐ **weak**

TR 2

☐ **delicate**

TR 3

Check Your Understanding

A. Match each word with the correct description. Two descriptions will not be used.

1. _____ strong
2. _____ delicate
3. _____ weak

a. something that lasts a long time

b. the opposite of strong

c. something that does not break easily

d. something that is not immediately obvious

e. when something can break or damage easily

B. Choose the sentence that correctly uses the underlined word.

1. a. They chose a very <u>strong</u> wood to build the dining room table.

   b. The cup was so <u>strong</u> that it broke into many pieces

2. a. The weather was <u>weak</u>, so they decided to stay inside.

   b. The bench was <u>weak</u> and started to break when too many people sat on it.

3. a. The butterfly's wings are <u>delicate</u> and can break easily in your hands.

   b. The bookshelf was very <u>delicate</u> and could hold many heavy books.

Challenge Words

Check (✔) the words you already know.

☐ brittle   ☐ flimsy   ☐ frail   ☐ potent   ☐ sturdy

☐ durable   ☐ fragile   ☐ makeshift   ☐ ramshackle   ☐ subtle

38. Tossing and Catching

Check (✔) the words you already know. Then, listen and repeat.

Tracks 1–4

☐ **pass**

TR 1

Definitions

To **catch** an object means to take hold of it with your hands.

To **pass** an object means to give it to someone.

To **throw** something means to move your hand or arm quickly and let go of the object so that it moves through the air.

To **toss** something means to throw it.

☐ **toss**

TR 2

☐ **catch**

TR 3

☐ **throw**

TR 4

Check Your Understanding

A. Match each word to the correct description. One description will not be used.

1. _____ catch   a. to give an object to someone

2. _____ pass   b. to move an object quickly through the air

3. _____ throw   c. to turn over an object quickly so it is on its other side

4. _____ toss   d. to take hold of an object with your hands

                     e. to throw an object

B. Underline the correct word to complete each sentence.

1. Ken picked up the baseball and (**tossed** / **passed**) it into the air.

2. Linda liked to (**throw** / **catch**) a tennis ball for her dog to catch in his mouth.

3. When her uncle threw the football, Amy tried to (**catch** / **toss**) it.

4. Please (**pass** / **throw**) me that glass of water.

Challenge Words

Check (✔) the words you already know.

☐ cast	☐ flick	☐ flip	☐ hurl	☐ snag
☐ chuck	☐ fling	☐ heave	☐ pitch	☐ thrust

138

39. Ascending Motion

Check (✔) the words you already know. Then, listen and repeat.

Tracks 1–6

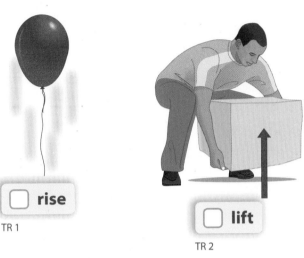

☐ **rise**

TR 1

☐ **lift**

TR 2

Definitions

To **climb** means to move toward the top of something.

To **lift** something means to take it and move it upward.

When you arrange things in a particular **order**, you put one thing first, another thing second, another thing third, and so on.

To **raise** something means to move it upward.

To **rank** someone or something means to place it in a particular position among a group.

When something **rises**, it moves upward.

☐ **climb**

TR 3

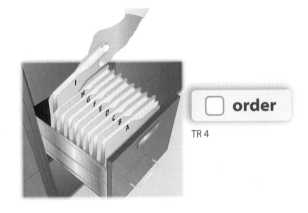

☐ **order**

TR 4

☐ **raise**

TR 5

RANKINGS OF RUNNERS	
1	TINA PEREZ
2	ROSIE SMITH
3	MARTA ARAS
4	JOHN SMITH

☐ **rank**

TR 6

Check Your Understanding

A. Match each description to the correct word. One description will take two words. One word will not be used.

1. _____ a particular sequence: one thing first, another second, and so on

2. _____ to move upward

3. _____ to place in a particular position in a group

4. _____ to move toward the top of something

5. _____ to move something upward

a. pry

b. order

c. climb

d. rise

e. raise

f. lift

g. rank

B. Circle the word that could replace the underlined phrase in the sentence without changing its meaning.

1. The moon <u>moves upward</u> in the sky.

   a. rises   b. orders   c. ranks

2. Harriet <u>arranged in a particular order</u> her top ten favorite movies.

   a. raised   b. ranked   c. lifted

3. Isaac <u>moved toward the top of</u> the stairs.

   a. lifted   b. ranked   c. climbed

4. If you know the answer to the question, <u>move up</u> your hand.

   a. raise   b. climb   c. rank

5. The songs were put into <u>a particular arrangement</u> from shortest to longest.

   a. rise   b. order   c. climb

6. He grabbed the weights and <u>raised</u> them over his head.

   a. climbed   b. lifted   c. *a* and *b*

Challenge Words

Check (✔) the words you already know.

☐ arise   ☐ blast-off   ☐ hoist   ☐ mount   ☐ rate

☐ ascend   ☐ elevate   ☐ load   ☐ pry

40. The Act of Occurring

Check (✔) the words you already know. Then, listen and repeat.

Tracks 1–4

☐ use
TR 1

☐ do
TR 2

To clean the house, I will **use** the vacuum and **do** the dishes.

Definitions

To **do** something means to take action or to perform an activity or task.

To **happen** means to take place without being planned.

To **occur** means to happen.

To **use** something means to do something with it.

☐ happen
☐ occur

TR 3 and TR 4

Check Your Understanding

A. Choose the correct word from the word bank to complete each sentence. Two words will not be used.

do	**used**	**reaction**
apply	**happened**	**occur**

1. The rainstorm _____ very quickly and my books got all wet.

2. When the doctor saw his patient, he knew exactly what to _____ .

3. A car crash will _____ if you don't stop at the red light.

4. Andrea _____ the broom to sweep the kitchen floor.

B. Choose the sentence that correctly uses the underlined word.

1. a. Amy likes to <u>do</u> laundry on Sundays.

   b. I'm tired. I think I'll lie down and <u>do</u> for an hour.

2. a. The hungry children sat down to <u>use</u> the sandwiches.

   b. Robert is going to <u>use</u> a blender to make a strawberry milkshake.

3. a. Ben wondered what <u>happened</u> to the rest of his team members.

   b. The rabbit <u>happened</u> away very quickly.

4. a. The doctor performed an operation to try to <u>occur</u> his patient.

   b. April wanted to know when the accident <u>occurred</u>.

Challenge Words

Check (✔) the words you already know.

- ☐ apply
- ☐ commit
- ☐ function
- ☐ react
- ☐ reaction
- ☐ undergo

44. Giving and Taking

Check (✔) the words you already know. Then, listen and repeat.

Tracks 1–16

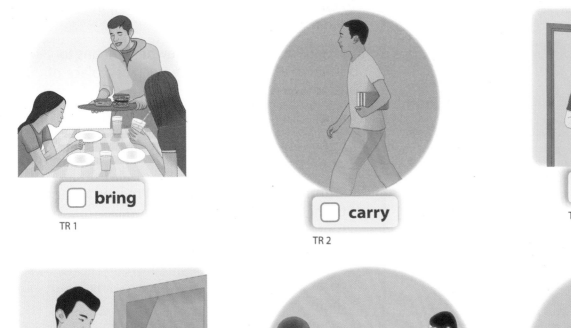

☐ **bring**

TR 1

☐ **carry**

TR 2

☐ **deliver**

TR 3

☐ **get**

TR 6

☐ **give**

TR 7

☐ **mail**

TR 8

☐ **move**

TR 11

☐ **place**
☐ **put**

TR 12 and TR 13

☐ **present**

TR 14

☐ **return**
TR 4

☐ **send**
TR 5

☐ **set**
TR 9

☐ **bear**
TR 10

☐ **remove**
TR 15

☐ **take**
TR 16

Definitions

To **bear** something means to carry it from one place to another.

If you **bring** something with you when you come to a place, you have it with you.

To **carry** something means to hold it in your hand and take it with you.

To **deliver** something somewhere means to bring it to a particular place, such as a place of business or a home.

To **get** something means to buy it or obtain it.

To **give** someone something means you let that person have it.

To **mail** something to someone means to send it to that person by mail.

To **move** something means to put it in a different place.

To **place** something somewhere means to put it there.

To **present** something to someone means to give it to that person formally.

To **put** something in a particular place or position means to move it into that place or position.

To **remove** something from a place means to take it away.

To **return** something that you borrowed or took means to give it back or put it back.

When you **send** someone a message or a package, you make it go to that person.

To **set** something somewhere means to put it there carefully.

To **take** something means to hold it or remove it.

Check Your Understanding

A. Underline the correct word to complete each sentence.

1. Alex was told to (**present / carry**) some wood into the house.

2. She walked into the kitchen to (**get / set**) a snack.

3. Please (**remove / bring**) a glass of water to me.

4. Laura is going to (**return / put**) her books to the library because they are due today.

5. Eric decided to (**mail / take**) a box of doughnuts to work.

6. Mrs. Jones had to (**present / move**) the award to the winner.

7. Every week, Karen (**moves / gives**) her son a few dollars to spend.

8. Mike drove to the post office to (**mail / place**) a package.

9. Sylvie will (**send / put**) a card to her aunt who is sick in the hospital.

10. My mom likes to (**take / place**) a small vase of fresh flowers on her desk.

11. Many restaurants will (**present / deliver**) food to your home.

12. The librarian (**sent / put**) all the books back on the shelves.

13. It was time to (**remove / set**) the old wallpaper from the walls.

14. Carefully, Ann (**gave / set**) her cup of hot chocolate on the table.

15. Before he (**moved / carried**) his car, he unloaded all the bags of groceries.

16. The donkey had to (**set / bear**) a heavy load of bricks.

B. Circle the word that could replace the underlined word or phrase in the sentence without changing its meaning.

1. Joe could not remember where he <u>placed</u> the remote control.

   a. took   b. put   c. presented

2. What will you <u>have with you when you come</u> to the picnic?

   a. bring   b. send   c. remove

3. The mayor <u>formally gave</u> a medal to the police officer for saving the little girl.

   a. mailed   b. delivered   c. presented

4. Irena <u>held and took</u> her books to class.

   a. sent   b. carried   c. set

5. Susan decided to <u>offer</u> her sister all of her old books.

   a. give   b. place   c. mail

6. Tina is wrapping a package for her uncle which she will <u>make go</u> to him.

   a. bring   b. send   c. place

7. Peter went to the bakery to <u>obtain</u> some fresh bread.

   a. remove   b. set   c. get

8. Angela <u>put</u> the dirty plates and glasses in the sink.

   a. carried   b. placed   c. sent

9. His job is to <u>take to a particular place</u> the letters and packages.

   a. deliver   b. return   c. put

10. She <u>sent through the mail</u> a birthday card to her best friend.

    a. placed   b. set   c. mailed

11. My neighbor <u>gave back</u> the shovel he borrowed.

    a. moved   b. set   c. returned

12. Josh <u>put in a different place</u> his dirty boots.

    a. brought   b. moved   c. presented

13. Andy <u>removed</u> his jacket from the coat closet.

    a. took   b. placed   c. put

14. You need to <u>take away</u> the dishes from the table.

    a. remove   b. set   c. put

15. Paul was asked to <u>carefully place</u> the crystal vase on the table.

    a. return   b. mail   c. set

16. On the hiking trip, Steven has to <u>carry from one place to another</u> a 40-pound backpack.

    a. bear   b. send   c. remove

Challenge Words

Check (✔) the words you already know.

☐ deposit   ☐ export   ☐ import   ☐ rid   ☐ supply
☐ eliminate   ☐ fetch   ☐ provide   ☐ ship   ☐ transfer

66. Coming / Going (General)

Check (✔) the words you already know. Then, listen and repeat.

 Tracks 1–14

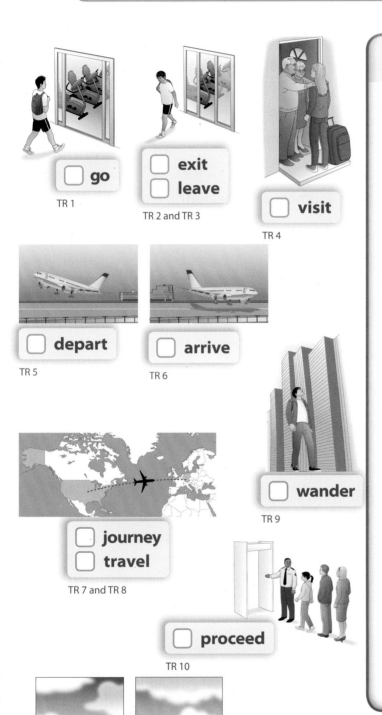

☐ **go**
TR 1

☐ **exit**
☐ **leave**
TR 2 and TR 3

☐ **visit**
TR 4

☐ **depart**
TR 5

☐ **arrive**
TR 6

☐ **wander**
TR 9

☐ **journey**
☐ **travel**
TR 7 and TR 8

☐ **proceed**
TR 10

☐ **appear**
TR 11

☐ **disappear**
TR 12

☐ **approach**
☐ **come**
TR 13 and TR 14

Definitions

To **appear** means someone or something becomes possible to see.

To **approach** something means to move closer to it.

To **arrive** somewhere means to reach a place or destination.

To **come** means that you arrive somewhere or that someone or something moves toward you.

To **depart** means to leave.

To **disappear** means to go out of sight.

To **exit** a place means to leave it.

To **go** somewhere means to move or travel there.

To **journey** somewhere means to take a long trip.

To **leave** a place or a person means to go away from that place or person.

To **proceed** to do something means to continue to do it after a brief pause.

To **travel** means to go from one place to another, often to a place that is far away.

To **visit** means to go to a place and stay for a time.

To **wander** means to walk around without a fixed plan or goal.

Check Your Understanding

A. Underline the correct word to complete each sentence.

1. A family (**exited / came**) into the library to borrow some books.

2. The train will (**depart / visit**) from the station at exactly 2:45.

3. When he was a young man, Nathan (**approached / traveled**) all around the world.

4. My neighbors (**visited / disappeared**) the Grand Canyon.

5. To avoid the crowds of people in front of the building, the movie star (**traveled / exited**) through the back door.

6. I heard a knock on my door, and then my mother (**journeyed / appeared**) in the doorway to my room.

7. We (**wandered / exited**) around the park for about an hour.

8. When Cynthia (**disappeared / approached**) her house, she noticed that she did not have her keys.

9. Jeff quickly (**left / arrived**) the room before anyone noticed.

10. Angie (**goes / departs**) to the same coffee shop every morning before work.

11. My cousins just (**left / arrived**) from out of town.

12. Evan (**journeyed / wandered**) from Los Angeles to Miami by plane.

13. Please (**proceed / left**) down the hallway until you see a door on the left.

14. Carmen's dog ran down the street and (**disappeared / visited**) around the corner.

B. Write the words from the word bank in the correct column. Some words can be used more than once.

exit	depart	leave	travel	go
come	journey	appear	arrive	visit
approach	proceed	wander	disappear	

TO MOVE AWAY	TO MOVE TOWARD

Challenge Words

Check (✔) the words you already know.

☐ access   ☐ adventure   ☐ dissolve   ☐ oncoming   ☐ stray

☐ advance   ☐ departure   ☐ migrate   ☐ roam   ☐ tour

141. Descending Motion (General)

Check (✔) the words you already know. Then, listen and repeat.

 Tracks 1–6

☐ **drop**
TR 1

☐ **fall**
TR 3

☐ **lay**
TR 4

☐ **tumble**
TR 2

Check Your Understanding

A. Match each word to the correct description. One description will not be used.

1. _____ dump
2. _____ lay
3. _____ fall
4. _____ slump
5. _____ tumble
6. _____ drop

a. to hang down loosely
b. to sit down suddenly and heavily
c. to move quickly toward the ground by accident
d. to put something down carefully
e. to fall with a rolling movement
f. to let something fall
g. to leave something quickly and without being careful

B. Circle the word that could replace the underlined phrase in the sentence without changing its meaning.

1. Sara released the ball and watched it <u>fall with a rolling movement</u> down the hill.

   a. drop   b. lay   c. tumble

2. Mary was so tired that she <u>sat heavily</u> into a comfortable chair.

   a. dumped   b. tumbled   c. slumped

□ **dump**

TR 5

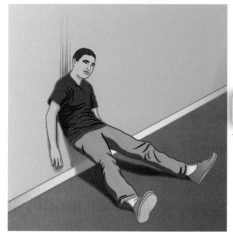

□ **slump**

TR 6

Definitions

To **drop** something means to let it fall.

To **dump** something somewhere means to put it there quickly and without being careful.

To **fall** means to move quickly toward the ground by accident.

To **lay** something somewhere means to put it there carefully.

To **slump** means to fall or sit down suddenly and heavily.

To **tumble** means to fall with a rolling movement.

3. If you <u>let fall</u> the tray of food, all the dishes will break.

    a. drop   b. lay   c. tumble

4. Tony <u>set down carefully</u> the bag of groceries on the kitchen table.

    a. dumped   b. fell   c. laid

5. Anita <u>dropped quickly</u> everything out of her purse to look for her keys.

    a. slumped   b. dumped   c. laid

6. During the windstorm, many branches and leaves <u>moved quickly toward the ground</u>.

    a. fell   b. laid   c. slumped

Challenge Words

Check (✔) the words you already know.

□ collapse   □ dip   □ plunge   □ slouch   □ tilt

□ descend   □ landslide   □ sag   □ swoop

147. Beginning Motion

Check (✔) the words you already know. Then, listen and repeat.

Tracks 1–5

☐ **begin**
☐ **start**

TR 1 and TR 2

☐ **try**

TR 3

Check Your Understanding

A. Match each word to the correct description. One description will not be used.

1. _____ beginning   a. to start doing something

2. _____ start   b. the first part of something

3. _____ origin   c. to do something that you were not doing before

4. _____ begin   d. the beginning part of a book that tells you what the book is about

5. _____ try   e. to make an effort to do something

        f. the point where a thing is created

B. Circle the word that could replace the underlined word or phrase in the sentence without changing its meaning.

1. From the <u>start of the event</u>, Alexander knew it would be a very bad day.

   a. beginning   b. try   c. begin

2. Mary <u>made an effort</u> to call her friend all afternoon, but he never answered the phone.

   a. began   b. tried   c. started

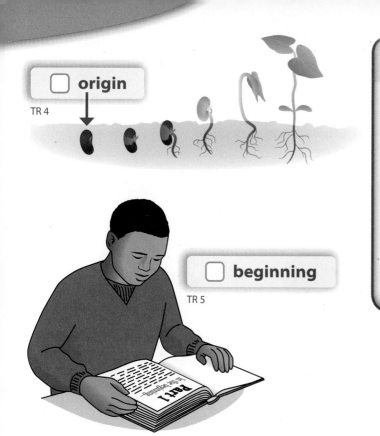

beginning

TR 5

Definitions

The **beginning** of something is the first part of it.

To **begin** something means to start doing it.

The **origin** is the point where something begins or is created.

If you **start** something, you do an action that you were not doing before.

If you **try** to do something, you make an effort to do it.

3. She needed to <u>begin</u> her homework before her mom came home from work.

   a. start   b. beginning   c. origin

4. Many people think that <u>the beginning of</u> salsa music was New York City.

   a. begin   b. origin   c. try

5. After she watched the news, Sandra <u>started doing something</u> to cook dinner for her family.

   a. origin   b. beginning   c. began

Challenge Words

Check (✔) the words you already know.

☐ embark   ☐ introduce   ☐ preface

☐ genesis   ☐ introduction   ☐ source

169. Lack of Motion

Check (✔) the words you already know. Then, listen and repeat.

☐ **rest**
☐ **relax**

TR 1 and TR 2

☐ **delay**

TR 3

DEPARTURES
3:00 NEW YORK DELAYED

☐ **stay**
☐ **remain**

TR 4 and TR 5

Check Your Understanding

A. Match each word to the correct description. One description will not be used.

1. _____ stay
2. _____ rest
3. _____ wait
4. _____ relax
5. _____ remain
6. _____ pause
7. _____ delay

a. to make someone or something late

b. to stop for a short time and then continue

c. to spend some time relaxing after doing something tiring

d. to continue to be in a place and not leave

e. to spend time doing very little until something happens

f. to feel calmer and less worried

g. to stay in a place and not move away

h. to say or do something that makes someone else stop what they are doing

B. Underline the correct word to complete each sentence.

1. Felix (**rested** / **delayed**) after working all morning in his garden.

2. Everyone left the restaurant while Trevor (**remained** / **rested**) to pay the bill.

DOCTOR'S OFFICE

Definitions

To **delay** means to make someone or something late, or to make a task take longer than expected.

If you **pause** while you are doing something, you stop for a short time and then continue.

If you **relax**, you stop work and feel calm and less worried.

If you **remain** in a place, you stay there and do not move away.

If you **rest**, you spend some time relaxing after doing something tiring.

If you **stay** where you are, you continue to be there and do not leave.

When you **wait**, you stay in a place and do very little until an event happens.

3. The company's president was late, so we (**delayed / remained**) the meeting for an hour.

4. It might help you to (**stay / relax**) if you take long, deep breaths.

5. We liked the city so much that we decided to change our travel plans and (**relax / stay**) one more night.

6. During her speech, Sharon (**stayed / paused**) for a moment before she continued speaking.

7. I'm going to be late, so don't (**wait / relax**) for me.

Challenge Words

Check (✔) the words you already know.

☐ await   ☐ hang   ☐ interrupt   ☐ linger   ☐ procrastinate

☐ dangle   ☐ hesitate   ☐ intervene   ☐ postpone   ☐ suspend

170. Descending Motion

Check (✔) the words you already know. Then, listen and repeat.

Tracks 1–5

☐ **lie**

TR 1

☐ **sit**

TR 2

Check Your Understanding

A. Choose the correct word from the word bank to complete each sentence. One word will not be used.

sat	lie	flop
kneel	crouch	squatted

1. The man _____ so he could put the little boy's shoes on.

2. Ben _____ in a comfortable chair and listened to his MP3 player.

3. Carlos decided to _____ on one knee when he asked Kayla to marry him.

4. The doctor told me to _____ still so he could check my pulse.

5. The little boy needed to _____ behind the sofa to hide from his sister.

☐ **crouch**

TR 3

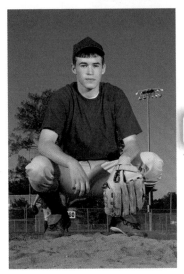

☐ **squat**

TR 4

Definitions

To **lie** somewhere means to rest your body in a flat position.

To **sit** means to place your bottom on a chair or on the ground with your back upright.

To **crouch** means to bend your legs so that you are close to the ground.

To **kneel** means to bend your legs and rest with one or both of your knees on the ground or floor.

To **squat** means to lower yourself toward the ground, balancing on your feet with your legs bent.

☐ **kneel**

TR 5

B. Write **T** for **true statements** and **F** for **false statements**.

1. _____ Most people crouch when they sleep.

2. _____ It is common to lie down when you want to rest.

3. _____ When you squat, you place your feet far apart and wave your arms.

4. _____ Students usually sit at their desks while in class.

5. _____ When you kneel, your weight is on one or both knees.

Challenge Words

Check (✔) the words you already know.

☐ flop   ☐ sprawl   ☐ stoop

182. Pulling and Pushing

Check (✔) the words you already know. Then, listen and repeat.

Tracks 1–6

☐ yank
TR 1

☐ pull
TR 2

☐ drag
TR 3

☐ push
TR 5

Check Your Understanding

A. Underline the correct word to complete each sentence.

1. Yolanda (**shoved / yanked**) the cord to turn on the ceiling fan.

2. The soccer fans were (**dragging / shoving**) each other to get a better view of the game.

3. Andrew had to (**drag / yank**) the heavy trash cans to the sidewalk.

4. Sara (**hauled / pulled**) the blanket over her head and went back to sleep.

5. When Richard's car ran out of gas, his friends (**yanked / pushed**) it down the street.

6. The delivery men (**yanked / hauled**) the heavy refrigerator up the stairs.

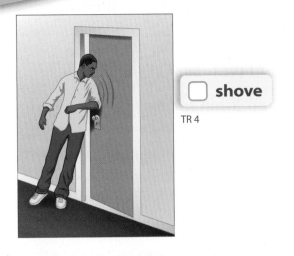

☐ **shove**

TR 4

Definitions

To **drag** something means to pull it along the ground.

To **haul** something somewhere means to move it using a lot of effort.

To **pull** something means to hold it firmly and use force to move it.

To **push** something means to use force to make it move forward or away from you.

To **shove** something means to push it roughly.

To **yank** something means to pull it hard.

☐ **haul**

TR 6

B. Write **T** for **true statements** and **F** for **false statements**.

1. _____ Hauling something is hard work.

2. _____ It is generally polite to shove someone.

3. _____ When you push something, you are moving it toward you.

4. _____ If you yank someone's arm, you touch it softly.

5. _____ When you drag something, it is touching the ground.

6. _____ When you pull something, you are putting it down on the ground.

Challenge Words

Check (✔) the words you already know.

☐ gravity   ☐ insert   ☐ propel

☐ inject   ☐ lug   ☐ tow

199. Angular and Circular Motions

Check (✔) the words you already know. Then, listen and repeat.

Tracks 1–11

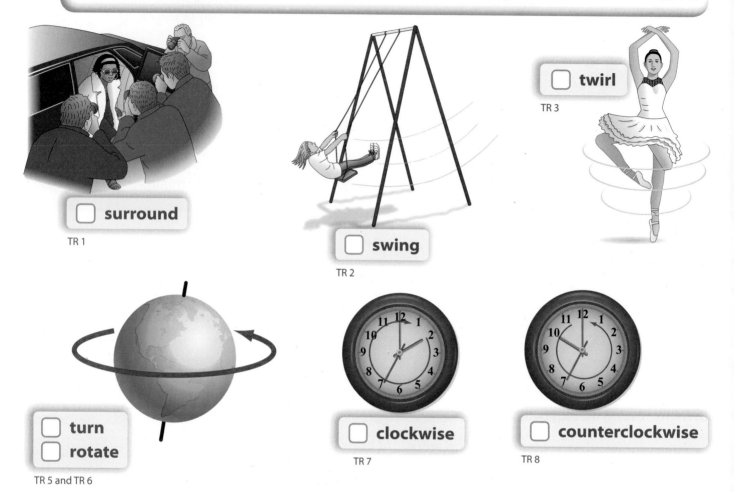

☐ **surround**

TR 1

☐ **swing**

TR 2

☐ **twirl**

TR 3

☐ **turn**
☐ **rotate**

TR 5 and TR 6

☐ **clockwise**

TR 7

☐ **counterclockwise**

TR 8

Check Your Understanding

A. Underline the correct word to complete each sentence.

1. The soccer ball (**around / rolled**) out of the yard and onto the sidewalk.

2. Max tried to (**twist / swing**) the jar lid, but it was stuck.

3. The hip-hop dancer began to (**counterclockwise / spin**) on his head.

4. A wooden fence (**surrounds / turns**) Kendra's entire backyard.

5. The mechanic said that I should (**clockwise / rotate**) my car's tires every year.

around

TR 4

roll

TR 9

spin

TR 10

twist

TR 11

Definitions

Things or people that are **around** a place or object surround it or are on all sides of it.

When something is moving **clockwise**, it is moving in the same direction as the hands on a clock move.

Something that moves **counterclockwise** moves in the direction opposite to which the hands of a clock move.

To **roll** something means to move it along a surface, turning it over many times.

When something **rotates**, it turns in a circle around a central line or point.

To **spin** an object means to turn it quickly around a central point.

If an item **surrounds** you, it is on every side of you or it is in a circle around you.

To **swing** something means to move it repeatedly backward and forward or from side to side through the air.

When something **turns**, it moves around in a circle.

To **twirl** something means to turn it around several times very quickly.

If you **twist** something, you turn it in a circular motion with your hands.

6. Sandra likes to (**twirl** / **around**) her hair on her finger.

7. When Andy walks, he (**swings** / **surrounds**) his arms back and forth.

8. Marie turned the key (**roll** / **counterclockwise**) to open the door.

9. Oliver (**turned** / **surrounded**) the screwdriver three times to tighten the screw.

10. The man planted flowers all (**rotate** / **around**) his house.

11. The hands of a clock move (**swing** / **clockwise**).

B. Write **T** for **true statements** and **F** for **false statements**.

1. _____ When an object spins, it changes direction.

2. _____ Something that is rolling is turning over many times.

3. _____ Something that is moving counterclockwise is moving in the same direction as the hands on a clock.

4. _____ When you twist something, your body spins but the object stays still.

5. _____ If an object is turning in a circle around a central line, we say it is rotating.

6. _____ Something that is moving clockwise is moving in the same direction as the hands on a clock.

7. _____ If people are around you, they are on your left side only.

8. _____ When something swings, it moves through the air.

9. _____ Twirling is the same as rolling.

10. _____ When a car turns, it stops moving.

11. _____ If trees surround your house, they are on all sides of it.

Challenge Words

Check (✔) the words you already know.

- ☐ circulation
- ☐ orbit
- ☐ recoil
- ☐ revolve
- ☐ swirl
- ☐ invert
- ☐ reciprocal
- ☐ reverse
- ☐ swerve
- ☐ whirl

215. Completion

Check (✔) the words you already know. Then, listen and repeat.

 Tracks 1–4

Definitions

To **complete** a task means to finish it.

To **end** means to stop an activity.

To **finish** doing something means to stop doing it.

The **last** thing, person, event, or period of time is the one that happens or comes after all the others.

☐ **end**
☐ **finish**

TR 1 and TR 2

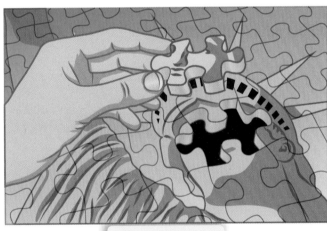

☐ **complete**

TR 3

☐ **last**

TR 4

Check Your Understanding

A. Match each word to the correct description. One description will not be used.

1. _____ end
2. _____ complete
3. _____ finish
4. _____ last

a. to stop doing something when everything is done

b. a time or date before which a piece of work must be finished

c. the thing that happens after all the others

d. to stop an activity

e. to finish a task

B. Underline the correct word to complete each sentence.

1. The (**last** / **complete**) ten minutes of the movie was the best part.

2. Ted needed to (**complete** / **end**) his phone conversation because he was getting into his car.

3. Everyone applauded when the mayor (**last** / **finished**) speaking.

4. Mary took two years to (**end** / **complete**) her novel.

Challenge Words

Check (✔) the words you already know.

- ☐ accomplish
- ☐ completion
- ☐ deadline
- ☐ deed
- ☐ final
- ☐ fulfill
- ☐ graduate

216. Shifting Motion

Check (✔) the words you already know. Then, listen and repeat.

 Tracks 1–4

☐ **slip**

TR 1

Definitions

To **rock** means to move slowly backward and forward or side to side.

When something **skids**, it moves sideways or forward in a bumpy or sliding motion.

When someone or something **slides**, it moves smoothly over a surface.

If you **slip**, you accidentally slide and fall.

 ☐ **rock**

TR 2

☐ **slide**

TR 3

 ☐ **skid**

TR 4

Check Your Understanding

A. Match each word to the correct description. One description will not be used.

1. _____ slip

2. _____ rock

3. _____ skid

4. _____ slide

    a. to move smoothly over a surface

    b. to move sideways with a bumpy or sliding motion

    c. to accidentally slide and fall

    d. to move slowly backward and forward

    e. to move to a higher position

B. Underline the correct word to complete each sentence.

1. Kathy was careful not to (**slip / rock**) as she walked on the wet floor.

2. The car (**rocked / skidded**) quickly around the corner.

3. Michelle gently (**slipped / rocked**) back and forth in her chair.

4. Henry (**slid / skidded**) the water bottle across the table so that I could reach it.

Challenge Words

Check (✔) the words you already know.

☐ shift   ☐ sway

166

247. Joining

Check (✔) the words you already know. Then, listen and repeat.

Tracks 1–11

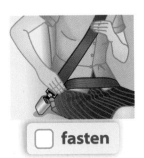

☐ **fasten**

TR 1

☐ **include**

TR 2

Batteries included!

☐ **stick**

TR 3

☐ **marriage**
☐ **marry**
☐ **wedding**

TR 4, TR 5, and TR 6

Definitions

To **attach** something means to fasten it to something else.

To **combine** means to join two or more things together.

To **connect** means to attach or join two things together.

To **fasten** something means to join or attach the two sides of an object or item together.

To **include** something means to make or insert it as part of something else.

To **join** two things means to attach or fasten them together.

A **marriage** is the time when two people get married.

To **marry** means two people legally become husband and wife in a special ceremony.

To **meet** means to join or come together.

To **stick** one thing to another means to join them together using glue or tape.

A **wedding** is a marriage ceremony and the party that often takes place after the ceremony.

☐ **attach**

TR 7

☐ **connect**
☐ **join**

TR 8 and TR 9

☐ **combine**

TR 11

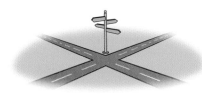

☐ **meet**

TR 10

167

Check Your Understanding

A. Underline the correct word to complete each sentence.

1. Thomas and Laura had a large (**wedding** / **connect**) at an elegant hotel.

2. Jim and Nancy have been (**married** / **marriage**) for 25 years.

3. Her grandmother (**marriage** / **joined**) the pieces of fabric together to make a skirt.

4. Darlene's new skirt (**combined** / **fastened**) in the back.

5. Jenny used glue to (**stick** / **marry**) the pictures in her scrapbook.

6. After watching Robbie play, John (**fastened** / **included**) Robbie on his basketball team.

7. He (**met** / **combined**) white paint with red paint to make a pink mixture.

8. Richard planned to (**meet** / **fasten**) his girlfriend for dinner.

9. The (**marriage** / **include**) of the prince and princess was watched on television by people all around the world.

10. Dennis tried to (**include** / **connect**) his new printer to the computer.

11. The heavy mirror was (**attached** / **combined**) to the wall with four large screws.

B. Circle the correct word to complete each sentence.

1. The price of your airplane ticket _____ a snack and drinks.

   a. includes   b. fastens   c. joins

2. Karen will _____ her mother for lunch at a café.

   a. connect   b. marry   c. meet

3. Kevin _____ the buttons on his jacket because he was cold.

   a. included   b. combined   c. fastened

4. Tyler _____ butter and sugar together to make frosting for the cupcakes.

   a. attached   b. combined   c. married

5. The seat covers were _____ to the chairs with elastic bands.

   a. attached   b. married   c. included

6. Steven attended his nephew's _____ at St. Paul's Cathedral.

   a. meet   b. marry   c. wedding

7. Andrew proposed to Carol, and they plan to _____ in six months.

   a. marry   b. combine   c. stick

8. At the time of their _____, Joan and Martin had not yet bought a home.

   a. fasten   b. join   c. marriage

9. Tim was having trouble _____ his computer to the Internet.

   a. including   b. connecting   c. combining

10. Teresa tried to _____ the two puzzle pieces together.

   a. join   b. meet   c. include

11. George needed to _____ stamps on the envelopes.

   a. marry   b. stick   c. meet

Challenge Words

Check (✔) the words you already know.

☐ accompany   ☐ connection   ☐ contain   ☐ intersect   ☐ link

☐ associate   ☐ consist   ☐ engage   ☐ involve   ☐ unite

280. Motion (General)

Check (✔) the words you already know. Then, listen and repeat.

Tracks 1–4

☐ **action**

TR 1

☐ **activity**

TR 2

Check Your Understanding

A. Choose the sentence that correctly uses the underlined word.

1. a. The wheel went around in a circular <u>motion</u>.

   b. Beth took the <u>motion</u> and put it in her coffee mug.

2. a. The children were glad that there was plenty of time for <u>play</u> after school.

   b. The <u>play</u> was about the size of a button.

3. a. We drove the <u>activity</u> across the country.

   b. There were many <u>activities</u> to choose from, such as riding bikes and drawing.

4. a. While the director was sick at home, there was little <u>action</u> at his office.

   b. Brooke stored the <u>action</u> in her garage.

☐ **play**

TR 3

☐ **motion**

TR 4

B. Underline the correct word to complete each sentence.

1. Pete planned an outdoor (**action** / **activity**) of rock climbing with his friends.

2. Leah let the children have an hour of (**play** / **motion**) before she put them to bed.

3. The (**motion** / **activity**) of the cradle gently rocking put the baby to sleep.

4. She watched the baseball game closely so she wouldn't miss the (**play** / **action**) on the field.

Challenge Words

Check (✔) the words you already know.

☐ kinetic   ☐ movable   ☐ portable

☐ mobile   ☐ osmosis   ☐ traffic

281. Vibration

Check (✔) the words you already know. Then, listen and repeat.

Tracks 1–5

☐ shake
TR 2

☐ wiggle
TR 3

☐ juggle
TR 1

Check Your Understanding

A. Match each word to the correct description. One description will not be used.

1. _____ wiggle

2. _____ shake

3. _____ juggle

4. _____ vibrate

5. _____ shiver

a. to throw and catch several things and try to keep them in the air

b. to shake because you are cold, frightened, or sick

c. to move quickly backward and forward or up and down

d. to move something from side to side in small, quick movements

e. to beat regularly with pain

f. to shake with repeated small, quick movements

shiver

TR 4

Incoming Call

555-1212

vibrate

TR 5

Definitions

If you **juggle,** you throw and catch several things repeatedly and try to keep them in the air.

If someone or something **shakes,** they move quickly backward and forward or up and down.

If you **shiver,** your body shakes because you are cold, frightened, or sick.

If something **vibrates,** it shakes with repeated small, quick movements.

If you **wiggle** something, you make it move up and down or from side to side in small, quick movements.

B. Underline the correct word to complete each sentence.

1. An earthquake makes the ground and buildings (**shake / juggle**).

2. The little girl climbed out of the pool and began to (**vibrate / shiver**) with cold.

3. Allen (**wiggled / juggled**) his toes to keep the blood circulating.

4. The music was so loud it made the walls (**shiver / vibrate**).

5. Oliver learned how to (**juggle / shake**) for the school talent show.

Challenge Words

Check (✔) the words you already know.

☐ jumble	☐ quiver	☐ shudder	☐ throb	☐ wobble
☐ quake	☐ scramble	☐ squirm	☐ vibration	

282. Jerking Motion

Check (✔) the words you already know. Then, listen and repeat.

Tracks 1–4

☐ **wag**

TR 2

☐ **snap**

TR 3

☐ **bounce**

TR 1

Check Your Understanding

A. Choose the correct word from the word bank to complete each sentence. One word will not be used.

jolted	fidgeted	wag	bounce	snapped

1. Bill _____ with his pen when he felt nervous at work.

2. My dog began to _____ her tail when she saw me.

3. Shari's sunglasses _____ when she sat on them.

4. The children wanted to see who could _____ the ball the highest.

B. Choose the sentence that correctly uses the underlined word.

1. a. Oscar <u>bounced</u> his favorite watch and baseball cap.

   b. The basketball <u>bounced</u> off the pole and landed in the crowd of people.

2. a. Leo kept washing and <u>wagging</u> the dishes.

   b. The dog's tail was <u>wagging</u> because he was happy.

☐ **fidget**

TR 4

Definitions

When an object such as a ball **bounces**, it hits a surface and quickly moves in a different and usually opposite direction.

To **fidget** means to move your body or hands because you are nervous or bored.

If something **snaps**, it breaks with a short, sharp noise.

When a dog **wags** its tail, it moves its tail repeatedly from side to side.

3. a. The movie was so long that many people <u>fidgeted</u> in their seats.

   b. A famous inventor just <u>fidgeted</u> a new idea that will make lots of money.

4. a. The winter storm caused many tree branches to <u>snap</u> and fall to the ground.

   b. The pillow <u>snapped</u> when it landed on the floor.

Challenge Words

Check (✔) the words you already know.

☐ bob   ☐ deflect   ☐ jerk   ☐ jounce   ☐ twitch

☐ budge   ☐ flounce   ☐ jolt   ☐ lurch

283. Expanding Motion

Check (✔) the words you already know. Then, listen and repeat.

Tracks 1–5

☐ **spread**

TR 1

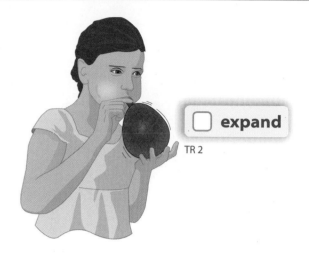

☐ **expand**

TR 2

Check Your Understanding

A. Choose the sentence that correctly uses the underlined word.

1. a. As he pumped air into the bicycle tire, it <u>expanded</u> slowly.

   b. The boss <u>expanded</u> all his workers to go home early.

2. a. Sandra used a microscope to <u>magnify</u> the parts of a cell.

   b. Denny <u>magnified</u> the soup until it was done.

3. a. My parents <u>blasted</u> the table to clean up after dinner.

   b. The miners tried to <u>blast</u> a hole in the side of the mountain.

4. a. She <u>spread</u> her newspaper all over the kitchen table.

   b. Tyler was dizzy because he <u>spread</u> round and round.

5. a. The artist <u>exploded</u> her painting in a frame to hang on the wall.

   b. During the attack, several bombs <u>exploded</u> in the battlefield.

Definitions

If you **blast** something, you destroy it by making it explode.

To **expand** means to become larger.

To **explode** means to burst with great force.

If you **magnify** something, you make it look larger than it really is.

If you **spread** something, you open or arrange it over a surface.

☐ **magnify**

TR 3

☐ **blast**
☐ **explode**

TR 4 and TR 5

B. Circle the correct answer to complete each sentence.

1. When you magnify something, it _____ .

   a. looks larger than it really is   b. bursts with great force

2. When something explodes, it _____ .

   a. bursts with great force   b. becomes larger in size

3. When you blast something, it _____ .

   a. becomes larger   b. explodes

4. When you spread something, you _____ .

   a. make it look larger than it really is   b. open it over a surface

5. If something expands, it _____ .

   a. looks larger than it really is   b. becomes larger in size

Challenge Words

Check (✔) the words you already know.

☐ burst   ☐ enlarge   ☐ extend   ☐ protrude   ☐ swell

☐ discharge   ☐ erupt   ☐ jut   ☐ scatter

300. Pursuit

Check (✔) the words you already know. Then, listen and repeat.

Tracks 1–3

☐ **chase**

TR 1

☐ **follow**

TR 2

Check Your Understanding

A. Choose the correct word from the word bank to complete each sentence. One word will not be used.

track	pursues	followed	chased

1. The visitors _____ the guide through the museum.

2. The police officer turned on her siren and _____ the car thief down the street.

3. Some hunters learn how to _____ animals by looking for foot prints.

track

TR 3

B. Circle the word that could replace the underlined words in the sentence without changing its meaning.

1. The scientists <u>followed signs of movement made by</u> the gorillas by looking carefully for broken tree branches.

   a. tracked   b. chased   c. followed

2. Tony and his classmates <u>walked behind</u> their teacher to the lunchroom.

   a. tracked   b. chased   c. followed

3. The children <u>ran after</u> the dog when it tried to run into the street.

   a. tracked   b. chased   c. followed

Challenge Words

Check (✔) the word if you already know it.

pursue

301. Reducing / Diminishing

Check (✔) the words you already know. Then, listen and repeat.

Tracks 1–5

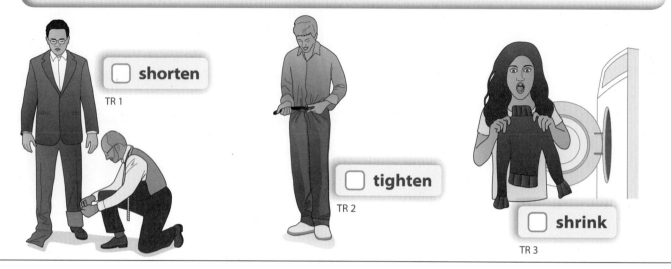

☐ shorten
TR 1

☐ tighten
TR 2

☐ shrink
TR 3

Check Your Understanding

A. Choose the correct word from the word bank to complete each sentence. One word will not be used.

crumpled	shrink	shortened
tightened	cramped	crumbled

1. Nancy _____ the ribbon by cutting the ends with scissors.

2. Conrad _____ the napkin and put it in his pocket.

3. I _____ the little girl's shoelaces so that they wouldn't come untied.

4. The bread _____ easily, so soon we had a pile of small crumbs.

5. When you cook spinach, the large leaves _____ and become much smaller.

B. Circle the word that could replace the underlined word or phrase in the sentence without changing its meaning.

1. Sean <u>fastened snugly</u> his seat belt by pulling on the strap.

    a. crumpled   b. shrank   c. tightened

2. Marjorie bit into the cupcake and it <u>broke into small pieces</u>.

    a. shortened   b. crumbled   c. shrank

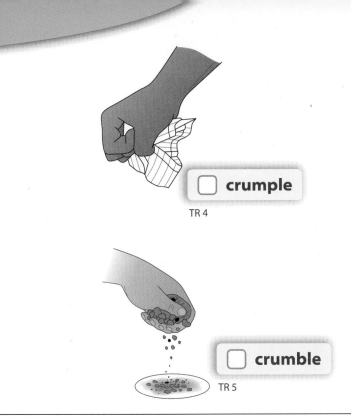

Definitions

To **crumble** means to break something into small pieces.

To **crumple** means to crush or press an object with your hand.

To **shorten** something means to make it shorter.

To **shrink** means to become smaller in size.

To **tighten** means to make something tighter.

☐ crumple
TR 4

☐ crumble
TR 5

3. Her dress had to be <u>made shorter</u> because it was dragging on the floor.

   a. crumbled   b. tightened   c. shortened

4. Rita <u>pressed</u> the paper into a ball and tossed it in the trash can.

   a. tightened   b. shrank   c. crumpled

5. Wool clothing <u>becomes smaller in size</u> if you put it in the dryer.

   a. shrinks   b. crumbles   c. shortens

Challenge Words

Check (✔) the words you already know.

☐ compress   ☐ cramp   ☐ diminish   ☐ reduce   ☐ wilt

☐ condense   ☐ crinkle   ☐ dwindle   ☐ shrivel   ☐ wither

302. Separating

Check (✔) the words you already know. Then, listen and repeat.

Tracks 1–3

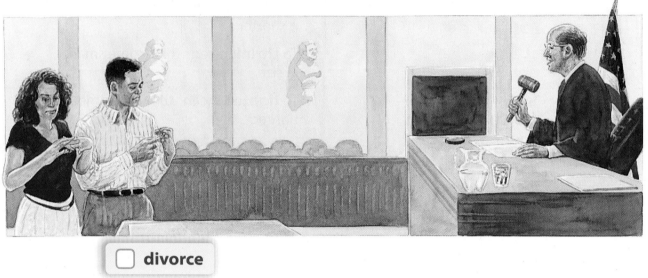

☐ **divorce**

TR 1

Check Your Understanding

A. Choose the correct word from the word bank to complete each sentence.

divorced	split	separate

1. Even though Valerie and Warren _____ the slice of pizza, each of them had enough to eat.

2. Rebecca and Jerry _____ last year because they did not get along.

3. It was difficult to _____ the pieces of paper because they were stuck together with glue.

B. Circle the word that could replace the underlined word or phrase in the sentence without changing its meaning.

1. The unhappy couple <u>legally ended their marriage</u> after being together for ten years.

   a. divorced   b. separated   c. split

Definitions

When a man and woman **divorce**, their marriage is legally ended.

If you **separate** people or things, you move them apart.

If something **splits**, it breaks into two or more parts.

☐ **separate**

TR 2

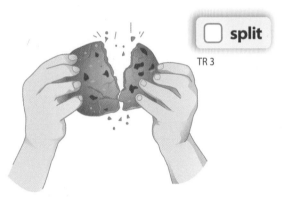

☐ **split**

TR 3

2. Doug <u>broke</u> his candy bar into parts to share with his brothers.

   a. divorce   b. separate   c. split

3. The teacher <u>moved apart</u> her students into six different groups.

   a. divorced   b. separated   c. split

Challenge Words

Check (✔) the words you already know.

☐ bisect   ☐ disconnect   ☐ ravel

☐ detach   ☐ divert   ☐ unwind

322. Opening and Closing

Check (✔) the words you already know. Then, listen and repeat.

Tracks 1–2

☐ open

TR 1

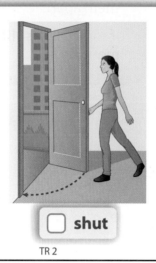

☐ shut

TR 2

Definitions

If you **open** something, you move it so that it is no longer covered or closed.

If you **shut** something, you close it.

Check Your Understanding

A. Choose the sentence that correctly uses the underlined word.

1. a. My mother <u>opened</u> her mouth to speak, but she was interrupted by the telephone ringing.
   b. During the storm, we made sure to <u>open</u> all the windows to keep the rain out.

2. a. After picking out her clothes, Janna <u>shut</u> the closet door.
   b. I <u>shut</u> the book and started to read the first chapter.

3. a. Roger didn't want to see what was inside the box, so he <u>opened</u> it.
   b. It was very hot in the classroom, so the teacher <u>opened</u> a few windows.

B. Choose the correct word from the word bank to complete each sentence. One word will not be used.

shut	gaped	opened
open	shutting	

1. When the doorbell rang, Irene _____ the front door.
2. When it began to rain, Eric _____ all the windows in his apartment.
3. Please _____ your books to page 118.
4. The plumber will be _____ off the water supply so that he can fix the leak.

Challenge Words

Check (✔) the words you already know.

☐ ajar   ☐ gape   ☐ restrict   ☐ shutdown

184

338. Halting Actions

Check (✔) the words you already know. Then, listen and repeat.

Tracks 1–2

☐ quit
TR 1

☐ stop
TR 2

Definitions

If you **quit**, you choose to stop doing an activity.

If you **stop** doing something, you end an activity or movement.

Check Your Understanding

A. Choose the correct word from the word bank to complete each sentence. One word will not be used.

| stop | restrained | stopped | quitting |

1. After 15 years as president of the company, my father is _____ his job to become a writer.
2. The umpire _____ the game when a player got hurt.
3. You need to _____ and think before you make a decision.

B. Choose the sentence that correctly uses the underlined word.

1. a. As part of his diet, Walter <u>quit</u> drinking soda.
   b. Sarah loved seeing her sister, so she decided to <u>quit</u> visiting her.

2. a. Marchella was thirsty, so she <u>stopped</u> drinking her water.
   b. When the car ran out of gas, it <u>stopped</u> moving.

3. a. Yolanda and Daniel want a large family, so they will <u>quit</u> having children after their first baby is born.
   b. After losing the election, Leo decided to <u>quit</u> politics.

Challenge Words

Check (✔) the words you already know.

☐ avoid   ☐ cancel   ☐ prevent   ☐ refrain   ☐ restrain

☐ barrier   ☐ obstacle   ☐ prohibit   ☐ resist   ☐ terminate

403. Force

Check (✔) the word if you already know it. Then, listen and repeat.

Track 1

Definition

To **force** means to use physical strength to make an item or a person move or fit somewhere.

☐ **force**

TR 1

Check Your Understanding

A. Write **T** for **true statements** and **F** for **false statements**.

1. _____ When you force something into a position, it does not take a lot of effort.

2. _____ If something is easy to move, you do not need to force it.

3. _____ When you force something, you are trying to move it.

B. Choose the sentence that correctly uses the underlined word.

1. a. I like to <u>force</u> grain to the sheep.

   b. The old window was difficult to move, but Don <u>forced</u> it closed.

2. a. At the concert, Cindy <u>forced</u> her way through the crowd and found a seat near the stage.

   b. It's important to <u>force</u> your teeth two times every day.

3. a. The boxes were big and heavy, but Alvin <u>forced</u> them to fit in his car.

   b. Yesterday I <u>forced</u> an interesting magazine.

Challenge Words

Check (✔) the words you already know.

☐ energy   ☐ pressure   ☐ propulsion

60. Places Related to Learning / Experimentation

Check (✔) the words you already know. Then, listen and repeat.

 Tracks 1–6

☐ **kindergarten**

TR 1

Definitions

A **classroom** is a room in a school where lessons take place.

Kindergarten is a class for children aged four and five years old.

A public **library** is a building where books and other reference materials are kept for people to use or borrow.

A **museum** is a place that shows rare, valuable, and important art and historical objects.

A **school** is a place where people go to learn.

A **schoolroom** is a classroom.

☐ **library**

TR 2

☐ **museum**

TR 3

☐ **classroom**
☐ **schoolroom**

TR 4 and TR 5

☐ **school**

TR 6

Check Your Understanding

A. Write **T** for **true statements** and **F** for **false statements**.

1. _____ A classroom would probably be found inside a bank.

2. _____ You probably would not find any teachers inside a schoolroom.

3. _____ Kindergarten is a class for science students.

4. _____ A school is a place where learning takes place.

5. _____ If you want to see interesting objects, you should go to a museum.

6. _____ A library is a good place to buy books, movies, and newspapers.

B. Underline the correct word to complete each sentence.

1. The (**classroom / museum**) had desks, computers, and textbooks in it.

2. Most of the children in the (**library / kindergarten**) class were five years old.

3. The art (**library / museum**) had paintings and sculptures made by my favorite artist.

4. The (**kindergarten / library**) has over 300,000 books for people to borrow.

5. At (**school / museum**) I learn new things, talk with my friends, and play sports.

6. When the bell rang, the students exited their (**schoolroom / museum**) and walked to their next class.

Challenge Words

Check (✔) the words you already know.

☐ academy   ☐ college   ☐ lab   ☐ planetarium   ☐ seminary

☐ campus   ☐ gallery   ☐ laboratory   ☐ schoolhouse   ☐ university

106. Places Related to Protection / Incarceration

Check (✔) the words you already know. Then, listen and repeat.

 Tracks 1–5

☐ **cage**
TR 1

Definitions

A **cage** is a structure made of metal bars where you keep animals.

A **cave** is a large hole in the side of a hill or under the ground.

A **fort** is a strong building that is used as a military base.

A **jail** is a place where criminals are kept as a punishment.

A **shelter** is a structure that protects you from bad weather or danger.

 ☐ **cave**
TR 2

☐ **fort**
TR 3

☐ **jail**
TR 4

☐ **shelter**
TR 5

189

Check Your Understanding

A. Match each word to the correct description. One description will not be used.

1. _____ jail
2. _____ shelter
3. _____ cave
4. _____ cage
5. _____ fort

a. a strong building that has military uses

b. a place where criminals are kept as a punishment

c. a small, locked room in a prison or a police station

d. a place that protects you from bad weather or danger

e. a large hole in a hillside or underground

f. a structure made of metal bars where you keep animals

B. Circle the word that could replace the underlined phrase in the sentence without changing its meaning.

1. Long ago, people lived in openings in the side of a hill.

   a. caves   b. jails   c. forts

2. The soldiers built a strong building that is used as a military base.

   a. jail   b. fort   c. cave

3. Charlene bought a structure with metal bars for her birds.

   a. fort   b. cage   c. shelter

4. As soon as he felt the winds of the hurricane, Harold ran for the place that provides protection.

   a. jail   b. fort   c. shelter

5. Many places where criminals have to stay are overcrowded.

   a. caves   b. jails   c. cages

Challenge Words

Check (✔) the words you already know.

☐ bunker   ☐ dungeon   ☐ garrison   ☐ outpost   ☐ quarantine

☐ cell   ☐ firehouse   ☐ haven   ☐ prison   ☐ stronghold

121. Places to Live

Check (✔) the words you already know. Then, listen and repeat.

Tracks 1–9

☐ castle
☐ palace

TR 1 and TR 2

☐ hotel

TR 3

☐ home
☐ house

TR 4 and TR 5

Definitions

An **apartment** is a room or set of rooms designed as a living space in a building or house.

A **castle** is a large building with thick, high walls that was built in the past to protect people from attack.

A **home** is the place where a person lives.

A **hotel** is a building with rooms that people can pay for and stay in when they are traveling.

A **house** is a building where people live.

A **hut** is a small, simple house or building.

A **motel** is a hotel next to a highway or road for people who are traveling by car.

A **palace** is a very large house where a king, a queen, or a president lives.

A **tent** is a movable shelter made of thick cloth held up by poles and ropes. You sleep in a tent when you go camping.

☐ hut

TR 6

☐ motel

TR 8

☐ tent

TR 7

☐ apartment

TR 9

Check Your Understanding

A. Match each word to the correct description. One description will not be used.

1. _____ apartment
2. _____ house
3. _____ home
4. _____ castle
5. _____ hotel
6. _____ hut
7. _____ tent
8. _____ motel
9. _____ palace

a. a shelter made of cloth that you use while camping
b. a hotel for people traveling by car
c. a very large house
d. a large building with thick, high walls
e. a group of rooms designed as a living space
f. a building where people live
g. a building at a school or a university where students live
h. the house or apartment where someone lives
i. a small, simple building
j. a building where people pay to sleep when they are traveling

B. Choose the sentence that correctly uses the underlined word.

1. a. We couldn't drive the car because Holly lost her <u>motels</u>.
   b. We were tired from driving all day, so we stopped to get a room at a <u>motel</u>.
2. a. Bridget pulled the <u>tent</u> over her head and kept walking in the rain.
   b. Upon arriving at the campground, the first thing we did was set up the <u>tent</u>.
3. a. Besides having many luxurious rooms, the presidential <u>palace</u> had elegant gardens.
   b. The <u>palace</u> is one of my favorite places to buy books and magazines.
4. a. The <u>castle</u> had two layers and was covered in chocolate frosting.
   b. The thick stone walls of the <u>castle</u> were built more than 500 years ago.
5. a. We lived in a two-bedroom <u>apartment</u> on the fifth floor of the building.
   b. The <u>apartment</u> was the perfect place to sleep during our camping trip in the mountains.
6. a. Near the beach there was a grass <u>hut</u> where a man was selling cold drinks.
   b. We rode in the <u>hut</u> up to the eleventh floor of the building.
7. a. The <u>house</u> sailed across the ocean.
   b. I live with my parents in a small, yellow <u>house</u> that has a large yard.
8. a. Kevin decided to hang the <u>home</u> on the wall in the living room.
   b. I would like to welcome you to my <u>home</u>.
9. a. We enjoyed staying at the <u>hotel</u>, with its comfortable rooms and delicious restaurant.
   b. Carolyn jumped in the <u>hotel</u> and started to swim.

Challenge Words

Check (✔) the words you already know.

☐ barracks   ☐ cottage   ☐ estate   ☐ inn   ☐ villa
☐ cabin   ☐ dormitory ☐ habitat ☐ mansion

190. Places Related to Sports / Entertainment

Check (✔) the words you already know. Then, listen and repeat.

Tracks 1–4

☐ **theater**

TR 1

Definitions

A **court** is an area marked off for playing sports such as tennis or basketball.

A **gym** is a club, building, or large room with equipment for doing physical exercises.

A **stadium** is a large sports or playing area with rows of seats inside of it.

A **theater** is a place where you go to see plays, shows, and movies.

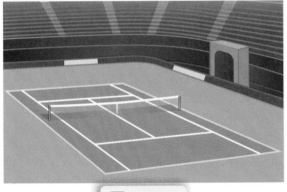

☐ **court**

TR 2

☐ **gym**

TR 3

☐ **stadium**

TR 4

Check Your Understanding

A. Choose the sentence that correctly uses the underlined word.

1. a. The <u>stadium</u> was able to fly over the mountains.

    b. The <u>stadium</u> was so large that we had a hard time finding our seats.

2. a. We ordered our food at the <u>theater</u> and ate it in the park.

    b. The movie was so popular that there was a long line of people at the <u>theater</u> entrance.

3. a. Lindsay and I met at the <u>court</u> to watch a tennis match.

    b. The <u>court</u> went in circles and eventually flowed down the drain.

4. a. Jon loved to run and exercise at the <u>gym</u>.

    b. Rita bought popcorn at the <u>gym</u> before the movie started.

B. Choose the correct word from the word bank to complete each sentence. One word will not be used.

theater	stadium	opera	courts	gym

1. At the park, both of the _____ were being used by the high

    school basketball team.

2. The _____ was filled with baseball fans that were excitedly

    waiting for the game to start.

3. I prefer to watch movies at a small, local _____ .

4. We lifted weights at the _____ for an hour.

Challenge Words

Check (✔) the words you already know.

☐ arena   ☐ coliseum   ☐ opera   ☐ rink

☐ auditorium   ☐ grandstand   ☐ playhouse

210. Places Where Goods Can Be Bought / Sold

Check (✔) the words you already know. Then, listen and repeat.

 Tracks 1–8

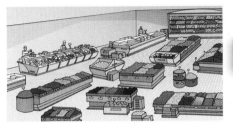

☐ **grocery**

TR 1

☐ **store**

TR 2

Definitions

A **bakery** is a place where bread, cakes, and pastries are baked and sold.

A **bookstore** is a shop where books are sold.

A **cafeteria** is a restaurant where you buy a meal and carry it to the table yourself. Places like hospitals, schools, and offices have cafeterias.

A **drugstore** is a store where medicines, makeup, and other beauty supplies are sold.

A **grocery** or a grocery store is a store that sells food.

A **lunchroom** is an area in a school or a business where students or employees can eat.

A **restaurant** is a place that serves food.

A **store** is a place where things are bought and sold.

☐ **bakery**

TR 3

☐ **bookstore**

TR 4

☐ **drugstore**

TR 5

☐ **cafeteria**
☐ **lunchroom**

TR 6 and TR 7

☐ **restaurant**

TR 8

Check Your Understanding

A. Match each word to the correct description. One description will not be used.

1. _____ restaurant
2. _____ drugstore
3. _____ bookstore
4. _____ store
5. _____ grocery
6. _____ bakery
7. _____ cafeteria
8. _____ lunchroom

a. a place where things are bought and sold

b. a place where you go to have your hair cut

c. a store that sells books

d. a place where bread and cakes are made

e. a store that sells medicines and makeup

f. a restaurant where you buy a meal and carry it to the table

g. the room at school or work where you eat

h. a place that serves food

i. a store that sells food

B. Underline the correct word to complete each sentence.

1. Dave went to the (**bookstore / bakery**) to look at magazines and buy a new novel.

2. In the (**drugstore / cafeteria**), I needed two trays to carry all the food to the table.

3. The (**grocery / bakery**) had all the types of food to buy that we needed for the weekend.

4. My cousin works in a (**lunchroom / store**) that sells clothing and shoes.

5. The smell of the freshly baked bread was coming from the (**bakery / bookstore**).

6. The coworkers agreed to meet in the (**drugstore / lunchroom**) at noon to eat together.

7. I need to stop at the (**drugstore / cafeteria**) to buy medicine.

8. My parents are going to have dinner at the new Thai (**lunchroom / restaurant**).

Challenge Words

Check (✔) the words you already know.

- ☐ booth
- ☐ café
- ☐ market
- ☐ pharmacy
- ☐ salon
- ☐ supermarket

321. Places Related to Meetings / Worship

Check (✔) the words you already know. Then, listen and repeat.

Tracks 1–3

☐ **church**

TR 1

Definitions

A **church** is a building where people go to pray.

A **shrine** is a religious place where people go to remember a holy person or event.

A **temple** is a building for worship.

☐ **temple**

TR 3

☐ **shrine**

TR 2

Check Your Understanding

A. Match each word to the correct description. Two descriptions will not be used.

1. _____ temple
2. _____ church
3. _____ shrine

a. where people go to remember a holy person or event

b. where a state's government meets

c. where people go to pray

d. where people worship

e. a large and important church

B. Write **T** for **true statements** and **F** for **false statements**.

1. _____ People cannot pray in a temple.

2. _____ A shrine is usually built to remember a religious song.

3. _____ Churches are places where you have a birthday party.

4. _____ Temples and churches are types of buildings.

Challenge Words

Check (✔) the words you already know.

☐ capitol   ☐ chapel   ☐ mission   ☐ synagogue

☐ cathedral   ☐ convent   ☐ monastery

324. Storage Locations

Check (✔) the words you already know. Then, listen and repeat.

Tracks 1–2

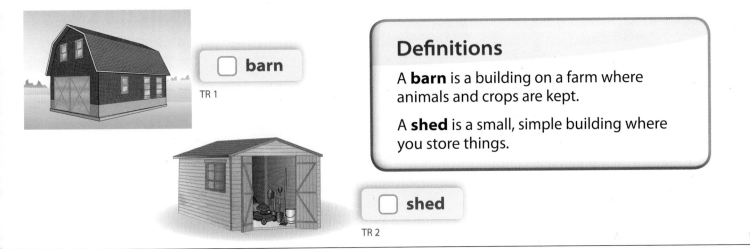

☐ **barn**

TR 1

☐ **shed**

TR 2

Definitions

A **barn** is a building on a farm where animals and crops are kept.

A **shed** is a small, simple building where you store things.

Check Your Understanding

A. Write **T** for **true statements** and **F** for **false statements**.

1. _____ Barns and sheds are both buildings.

2. _____ A barn can be found on a farm.

3. _____ Animals and crops are stored inside sheds.

B. Choose the sentence that correctly uses the underlined word.

1. a. The zookeeper put the lions, elephants, penguins, and monkeys in the <u>shed</u>.

   b. Dave looked in the <u>shed</u> for his fishing gear because he needed it for his trip.

2. a. Paul put out more straw in the <u>barn</u> for the horses, pigs, and other animals to sleep on.

   b. A <u>barn</u> is a great place to watch a play or movie.

3. a. When Anna's family comes to visit, they usually sleep in the <u>shed</u>.

   b. After riding their bicycles, Elizabeth and John put them in the <u>shed</u>.

Challenge Words

Check (✔) the words you already know.

☐ arsenal   ☐ hothouse   ☐ storeroom

☐ greenhouse   ☐ shack   ☐ warehouse

335. Places Related to Transportation

Check (✔) the words you already know. Then, listen and repeat.

Tracks 1–2

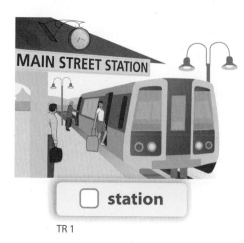

MAIN STREET STATION

☐ **station**

TR 1

☐ **airport**

TR 2

Definitions

An **airport** is a place where airplanes land and take off and where there are buildings and services for passengers.

A **station** is a place where trains stop so that people can get on or off.

Check Your Understanding

A. Underline the correct word to complete each sentence.

1. James went to the (**airport / station**) to watch the trains come and go.

2. The (**airport / station**) is a very busy place with planes landing and taking off.

3. Charlie likes to sit at the (**airport / station**) and imagine where all the travelers are going to fly next.

4. The train will stop at the next (**airport / station**).

B. Choose the sentence that correctly uses the underlined word.

1. a. We go once a week to the <u>station</u> to buy groceries.
   b. The train pulled slowly away from the <u>station</u>.

2. a. Adrian will arrive at the <u>airport</u> two hours before his flight to Greece leaves.
   b. An <u>airport</u> is an exciting place to grow up.

3. a. There was a fire at the <u>station</u>, so all the trains were delayed.
   b. If you use the <u>station</u> correctly, you'll get better grades at school.

Challenge Words

Check (✔) the words you already know.

☐ depot   ☐ hangar   ☐ terminal

364. Structures that Are Manmade

Check (✔) the words you already know. Then, listen and repeat.

Tracks 1–2

☐ tower

TR 1

Definitions

A **building** is a structure that has a roof and walls.

A **tower** is a tall, narrow building or a tall part of another building.

☐ building

TR 2

Check Your Understanding

A. Write **T** for **true statements** and **F** for **false statements**.

1. _____ A building has walls and a roof.

2. _____ A tower is an entrance to a structure.

3. _____ A tower is a tall structure that is usually wide.

4. _____ A building is a place where people can live or work.

B. Choose the sentence that correctly uses the underlined word.

1. a. There is a narrow <u>tower</u> on top of the school.

   b. Beverly decided to hang up the <u>tower</u> to dry in the sun.

2. a. Stephen picked up the <u>building</u> and put it in his pocket.

   b. Alicia lives on the first floor of the <u>building</u>.

3. a. Kathryn used the <u>tower</u> to cross the river.

   b. Once we reached the top of the <u>tower</u>, we had a nice view of the city.

4. a. Inside this <u>building</u>, you will find many offices and a small cafeteria.

   b. The boy held the <u>building</u> tightly in his hand so that it wouldn't blow away.

Challenge Words

Check (✔) the words you already know.

☐ construction ☐ silo ☐ skyscraper ☐ structure

365. Factories, Mills, and Offices

Check (✔) the words you already know. Then, listen and repeat.

Tracks 1–2

☐ **office**

TR 1

☐ **shop**

TR 2

Check Your Understanding

A. Choose the sentence that correctly uses the underlined word.

1. a. I went to the <u>shop</u> to brush my teeth and take a shower.

   b. After his bicycle was stolen, Samuel went to the <u>shop</u> to buy another one.

2. a. After lunch, Larry returned to his <u>office</u> to finish the project for the meeting.

   b. In her <u>office</u>, Heidi cooked all the food for her dinner party.

3. a. John's daughter was very sick, so he took her to the <u>shop</u>.

   b. Harry loved to take care of animals, so he went to the pet <u>shop</u> to buy some birds.

Definitions

An **office** is a place of business where people usually work at desks.

A **shop** is a small store that sells a particular type of thing.

B. Underline the correct word to complete each sentence.

1. The President of the United States has an (**office** / **shop**) in the shape of an oval.

2. That (**office** / **shop**) doesn't sell any shoes for children.

3. Each worker in this department has his own (**office** / **shop**) with a desk and a phone.

Challenge Words

Check (✔) the words you already know.

☐ factory   ☐ mill   ☐ studio   ☐ windmill

☐ headquarters   ☐ sawmill   ☐ treadmill   ☐ workshop

366. Ranches and Farms

Check (✔) the words you already know. Then, listen and repeat.

Tracks 1–2

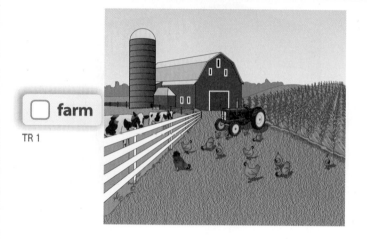

☐ **farm**

TR 1

☐ **ranch**

TR 2

Definitions

A **farm** is a piece of land, usually with a barn and other buildings, where people grow crops and keep animals.

A **ranch** is a very large farm used for keeping and raising animals.

Check Your Understanding

A. Write **T** for **true statements** and **F** for **false statements**.

1. _____ A ranch is a farm where flowers are grown.

2. _____ You will see animals and crops on a farm.

3. _____ Animals are found on farms and ranches.

B. Underline the correct word to complete each sentence.

1. Susan raises horses but does not grow any crops on her (**farm / ranch**).

2. The farmer raised chickens and grew crops on his (**farm / ranch**).

3. Martin lives on a (**farm / ranch**), where his family grows corn and wheat.

Challenge Words

Check (✔) the words you already know.

☐ dairy   ☐ plantation

399. Medical Facilities

Check (✔) the word if you already know it. Then, listen and repeat.

Track 1

Definition

A **hospital** is a place where doctors and nurses care for people who are sick or injured.

☐ **hospital**

TR 1

Check Your Understanding

A. Write **T** for **true statements** and **F** for **false statements**.

1. _____ If you are sick or injured, you should go to a hospital.

2. _____ A hospital is a good place to go dancing on a Saturday night.

3. _____ Nurses and doctors work at hospitals.

B. Choose a phrase from each column to create complete sentences. Write them below.

Ellen went	took the injured man	straight to the hospital.
The ambulance	to the hospital	rushed to the hospital.
He was injured	and had to be	to visit her sick friend.

1. _____

2. _____

3. _____

Challenge Words

Check (✔) the words you already know.

☐ clinic ☐ morgue ☐ mortuary ☐ ward

400. Monuments

Check (✔) the word if you already know it. Then, listen and repeat.

Track 1

Definition

A **monument** is something built to help people remember an important event or person.

☐ **monument**

TR 1

Check Your Understanding

A. Write **T** for **true statements** and **F** for **false statements.**

1. _____ A monument is a public way to remember a person who did something important.

2. _____ Monuments do not occur naturally. They are made by people.

3. _____ A monument is made for anyone who attends an important event.

B. Choose the sentence that correctly uses the underlined word.

1. a. The <u>monument</u> marked the birthplace of the famous painter.

   b. The creamy <u>monument</u> was eaten with a cup of hot coffee.

2. a. Taylor put on her <u>monument</u> before skiing down the hill.

   b. The stone <u>monument</u> took two years to complete.

3. a. There is a <u>monument</u> in the city center to remember the last battle of the war.

   b. Eli climbed on the <u>monument</u> and took a ride around the park.

Challenge Words

Check (✔) the words you already know.

☐ headstone   ☐ memorial   ☐ tomb   ☐ totem

☐ landmark   ☐ sphinx   ☐ tombstone

69. Emptiness and Fullness

Check (✔) the words you already know. Then, listen and repeat.

Tracks 1–4

☐ **empty**

TR 1

Definitions

If a container is **empty**, its contents have been removed.

If you **fill** a container or object with something, it becomes full.

If a container is **full**, it contains or holds as much of an object as it can.

Something that is **hollow** has an empty space inside it.

☐ **fill**

TR 2

☐ **full**

TR 3

☐ **hollow**

TR 4

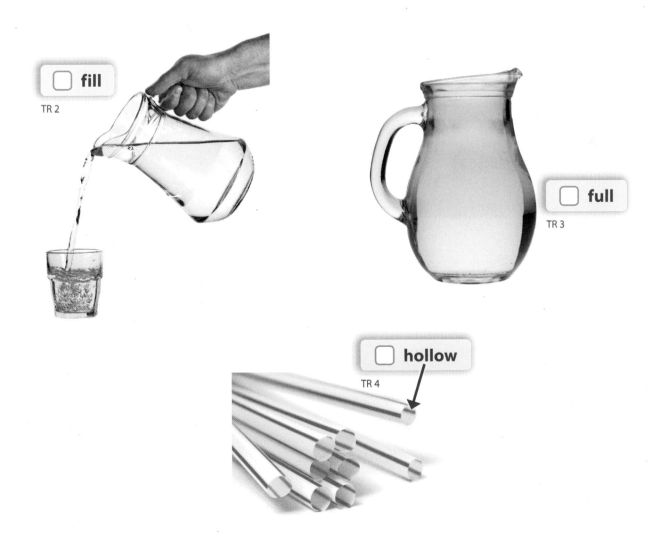

Check Your Understanding

A. Choose the sentence that correctly uses the underlined word.

1. a. Kara gave me an <u>empty</u> box to pack my stuff in.

   b. The <u>empty</u> refrigerator had milk, juice, eggs, and fruit in it.

2. a. At the restaurant, Joe and his friends <u>filled</u> their cups with ice and soda.

   b. When Sheila went to the park, she <u>filled</u> on the swings and slides.

3. a. Everyone says Spencer is <u>full</u> because he talks a lot.

   b. Fred's backpack has all of his textbooks in it, so it is <u>full</u>.

4. a. The family was <u>hollow</u> after taking a relaxing vacation.

   b. The tree trunk was <u>hollow</u>, so it was the perfect place for the birds to live.

B. Choose the correct word from the word bank to complete each sentence. One word will not be used.

| full | hollow | fill |
| empty | swollen | |

1. Abigail decided to _____ the bathtub with water so she could wash the dog.

2. My water bottle was _____ , so I went to get more water.

3. The chocolate eggs are very light and break easily because they are _____ .

4. The bowl was _____ . We could not put any more pasta in it.

Challenge Words

Check (✔) the words you already know.

☐ deflate   ☐ exhaust   ☐ null   ☐ swollen   ☐ void

☐ deplete   ☐ fraught   ☐ stuff   ☐ vacant

99. Dimensionality

Check (✔) the words you already know. Then, listen and repeat.

 Tracks 1–15

☐ **shallow**
TR 1

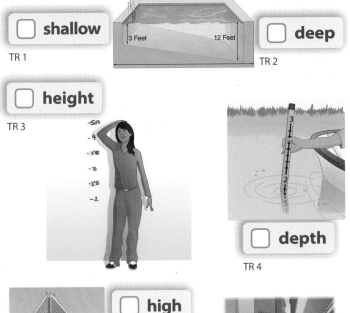
3 Feet   12 Feet

☐ **deep**
TR 2

☐ **height**
TR 3

☐ **depth**
TR 4

☐ **high**
☐ **tall**
TR 5 and TR 6

☐ **narrow**
TR 7

☐ **long**
TR 8

Definitions

When something is **deep**, it goes far below the surface of something.

The **depth** of something is how deep it is.

Height is the measurement from the bottom to the top of someone or something.

Something that is **high** extends a long way from the bottom to the top.

The **length** of something is its measurement from one end to the other.

Something that is **long** measures a great distance from one end to the other.

Something that is **narrow** is a small distance from one side to the other.

Something that is **shallow** is not deep.

Something that is **short** measures only a small amount from one end to the other.

The **size** of something is how big or small it is.

Something that is **tall** is higher than other things.

(Continued)

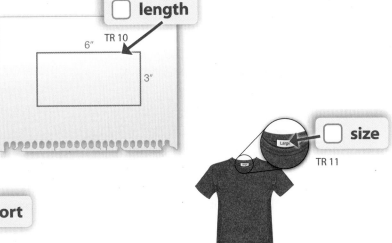

☐ **length**
TR 10
6"
3"

☐ **size**
TR 11

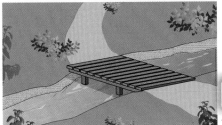

☐ **short**
TR 9

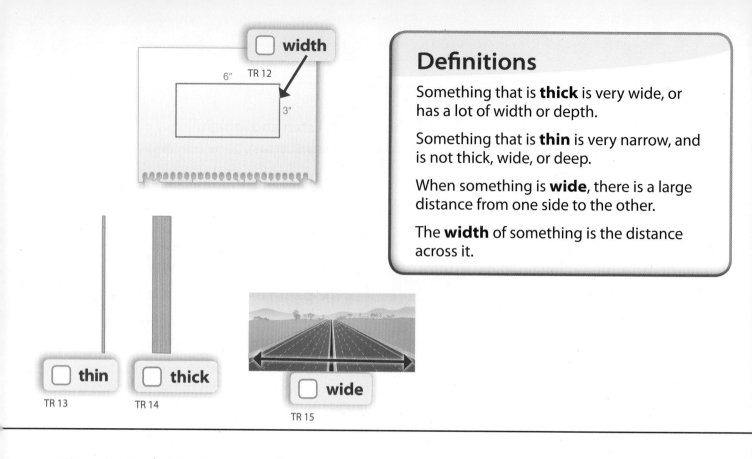

Definitions

Something that is **thick** is very wide, or has a lot of width or depth.

Something that is **thin** is very narrow, and is not thick, wide, or deep.

When something is **wide**, there is a large distance from one side to the other.

The **width** of something is the distance across it.

thin
TR 13

thick
TR 14

wide
TR 15

Check Your Understanding

A. Write **T** for **true statements** and **F** for **false statements**.

1. _____ Something that is short measures a small amount from one end to the other.

2. _____ If you stood in deep water, it would probably only cover your toes.

3. _____ Height measures the distance of something from bottom to top.

4. _____ Something that is thick has a small distance between one side and the other.

5. _____ When you refer to an object's size, you are talking about how big or small it is.

6. _____ *Narrow* is the opposite of *wide*.

7. _____ Depth measures how round something is.

8. _____ To find out an object's length, you need to measure from one end to the other.

9. _____ Something that is high has little distance from the bottom to the top.

10. _____ When figuring out an object's width, you measure its size from one side to the other.

11. _____ If a lake or river is very shallow, you cannot see the bottom.

12. _____ If a street is wide, there is plenty of space for cars.

13. _____ Something that is thin measures little from side to side.

14. _____ *Long* refers to a distance that is great.

15. _____ If you say something is tall, you are talking about its length.

B. Underline the correct word to complete each sentence.

1. There was a (**long / height**) line of people waiting to buy tickets.

2. Brandon paddled his boat across the (**size / deep**) part of the river.

3. When someone asks you how tall you are, they are asking about your (**short / height**).

4. Sandy and Debby didn't want to swim, so they were standing in the (**shallow / deep**) end of the swimming pool.

5. Karen measured the (**width / thick**) of her bookshelves to make sure they would fit in her new apartment.

6. These shirts come in three different (**sizes / heights**): small, medium, and large.

7. The statue in front of city hall is nearly 15 feet (**high / short**) and 10 feet wide.

8. The paper rips easily because it is very (**thin / high**).

9. Tony hiked along a (**tall / narrow**) path in the woods.

10. Paul measured the (**thick / length**) of the couch.

11. Angela cut the loaf of bread into (**deep / thick**) slices.

12. The freeway was (**wide / narrow**) enough for five lanes of traffic.

13. In some places, the (**depth / short**) of the ocean can be measured in miles.

14. Ethan is (**tall / thick**), so he can reach the books on the top shelf.

15. Mary walks to school because the school is a (**width / short**) distance from her house.

Challenge Words

Check (✔) the words you already know.

☐ broad	☐ dense	☐ extend	☐ measurement	☐ thickness
☐ deepen	☐ dimension	☐ layer	☐ scale	☐ trim

142. Rectangular / Square Shapes

Check (✔) the words you already know. Then, listen and repeat.

Tracks 1–7

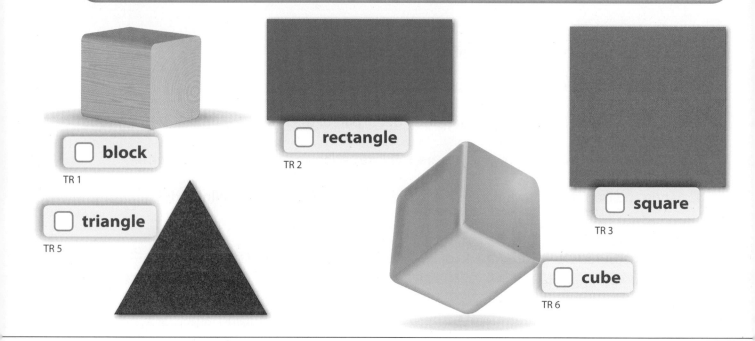

☐ **block**
TR 1

☐ **rectangle**
TR 2

☐ **square**
TR 3

☐ **triangle**
TR 5

☐ **cube**
TR 6

Check Your Understanding

A. Write **T** for **true statements** and **F** for **false statements**.

1. _____ Rectangles have straight sides.

2. _____ A cube is made up of four square surfaces.

3. _____ A triangular shape has curved sides.

4. _____ A block is a solid shape.

5. _____ Triangles have seven sides.

6. _____ A square has a pointy top.

7. _____ Pyramids have flat sides.

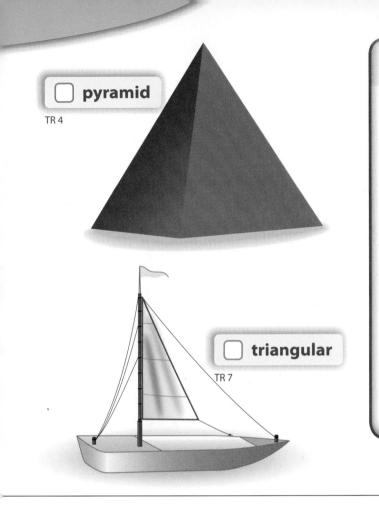

□ pyramid

TR 4

□ triangular

TR 7

Definitions

A **block** is a solid object that has six flat surfaces and a rectangular or cube-like shape.

A **cube** is a solid object with six square surfaces.

A **pyramid** is a solid shape with a flat base and flat sides that form a point where they meet at the top.

A **rectangle** is a shape with four straight sides.

A **square** is a shape with four straight sides that are all the same length.

A **triangle** is a shape with three straight sides.

Something that is **triangular** is shaped like a triangle and has three straight sides.

B. Match each word to the correct description. One description will not be used.

1. _____ triangular
2. _____ cube
3. _____ triangle
4. _____ square
5. _____ rectangle
6. _____ pyramid
7. _____ block

a. solid object with six square surfaces

b. solid shape with a flat base and flat sides that form a point at the top

c. solid object with flat surfaces and a rectangular or cube-like shape

d. shape with five straight sides

e. looks like a triangle

f. shape with four straight sides

g. shape with three straight sides

h. shape with four straight sides, all the same length

Challenge Words

Check (✔) the words you already know.

□ cubic   □ hexagon   □ parallelogram   □ polygon   □ quadrilateral

□ equilateral   □ octagon   □ pentagon   □ prism   □ trapezoid

193. Inclination

Check (✔) the words you already know. Then, listen and repeat.

Tracks 1–5

☐ **steep**

TR 1

☐ **even**
☐ **flat**
☐ **level**

TR 2, TR 3, and TR 4

Check Your Understanding

A. Match each word to the correct description. One description will not be used.

1. _____ steep   a. something that is level and smooth

2. _____ lean   b. when something bends from a vertical position

3. _____ flat   c. when a slope rises at a sharp angle

4. _____ even   d. a smooth and flat surface

5. _____ level   e. something that is straight and upright

                                  f. something that is horizontal or flat

□ **lean**

TR 5

Definitions

An **even** surface is smooth and flat.

A **flat** surface is level or smooth.

To **lean** is to bend or incline from a vertical position.

When something is **level**, it is horizontal or flat.

A **steep** slope rises at a very sharp angle.

B. Underline the correct word to complete each sentence.

1. The train struggled to climb up the (**steep** / **lean**) mountain.

2. The carpenter removed the bumps from the wood until the table's surface was completely (**even** / **steep**).

3. It was so windy that the small trees were (**flat** / **leaning**) over.

4. The top of my desk was not (**steep** / **level**), so my pencil kept rolling on to the floor.

5. My sister lives on the prairie where the land is (**flat** / **steep**). There aren't any trees or hills.

Challenge Words

Check (✔) the words you already know.

□ erect   □ incline   □ plumb   □ slant   □ tilt

218. Crookedness / Straightness

Check (✔) the words you already know. Then, listen and repeat.

Tracks 1–6

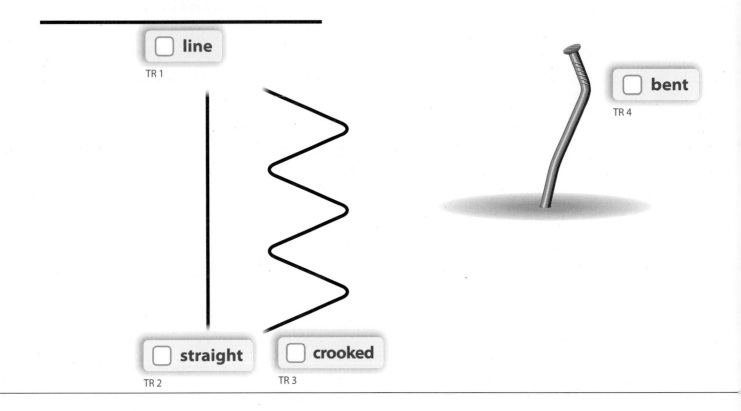

☐ line

TR 1

☐ bent

TR 4

☐ straight

TR 2

☐ crooked

TR 3

Check Your Understanding

A. Write T for true statements and F for false statements.

1. _____ Something that is straight has no curves in it.

2. _____ A bent object is one with many stripes on it.

3. _____ If something is crooked, it continues in one direction.

4. _____ A stripe is a band of color on the background of a different color.

5. _____ A cross is a mark that looks like the letter T.

6. _____ A line is a long, thick mark.

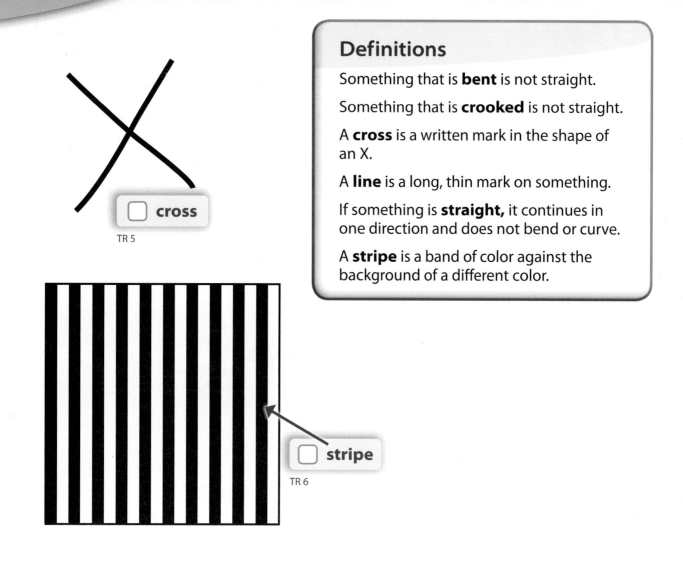

Definitions

Something that is **bent** is not straight.

Something that is **crooked** is not straight.

A **cross** is a written mark in the shape of an X.

A **line** is a long, thin mark on something.

If something is **straight,** it continues in one direction and does not bend or curve.

A **stripe** is a band of color against the background of a different color.

☐ cross

TR 5

☐ stripe

TR 6

B. Underline the correct word to complete each sentence.

1. Matilda's teeth were so (**straight / crooked**) that the dentist said it would take years to fix them.

2. It was so windy that many trees appeared to be (**bent / stripe**).

3. Julie wrote her name on the (**line / straight**).

4. The sailor painted a bright red (**stripe / bent**) on his boat to make it stand out.

5. The road was completely (**straight / crooked**), and there were no curves in sight.

6. You should mark your choice by making a (**bent / cross**) in the box.

Challenge Words

Check (✔) the words you already know.

☐ beeline   ☐ crisscross   ☐ strip   ☐ zigzag

217

270. Curved and Circular Shapes

Check (✔) the words you already know. Then, listen and repeat.

Tracks 1–9

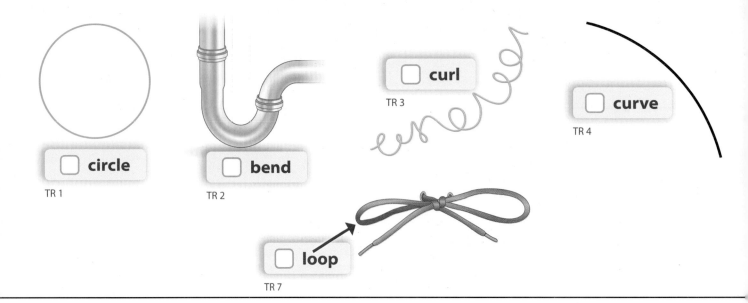

☐ **circle**

TR 1

☐ **bend**

TR 2

☐ **curl**

TR 3

☐ **curve**

TR 4

☐ **loop**

TR 7

Check Your Understanding

A. Match each word to the correct description. One description will not be used.

1. _____ circle

2. _____ loop

3. _____ bend

4. _____ cylinder

5. _____ curl

6. _____ curve

7. _____ twist

8. _____ oval

9. _____ round

a. a shape with one flat round end and one pointed end

b. when something is shaped like a ball

c. a shape like an egg

d. a round shape

e. something that forms a curved shape

f. a smooth, bent line

g. a shape like a circle in a piece of string

h. a shape with circular ends and long, straight sides

i. a curve or turn in a road

j. something that has been twisted

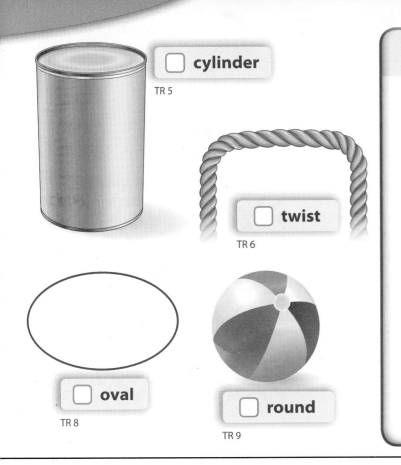

□ cylinder
TR 5

□ twist
TR 6

□ oval
TR 8

□ round
TR 9

Definitions

A **bend** in a road or a pipe is a curve or angle in it.

A **circle** is a round shape.

A **curl** of something is a piece or quantity of it that is curved or spiral in shape.

A **curve** is a smooth, gradually bending line; for example, part of the edge of a circle.

A **cylinder** is a shape or a container with circular ends and long, straight sides.

A **loop** is a shape like a circle in a piece of string or rope.

An **oval** is a shape that looks like an egg.

Something that is **round** is shaped like a circle or ball.

A **twist** is something twisted or formed by twisting.

B. Write **T** for **true statements** and **F** for **false statements**.

1. _____ A twist is similar in shape to an egg.

2. _____ A loop is a circular formation in a rope.

3. _____ If there is a bend in a road, then the road is not straight.

4. _____ A circle is a round shape with a pointy top.

5. _____ If someone's hair has curls, it means the hair has a spiral shape.

6. _____ Each end of a cylinder has a circular shape.

7. _____ A curve is a line without bends in it.

8. _____ An oval is a moon-shaped object.

9. _____ A ball has a round shape.

Challenge Words

Check (✔) the words you already know.

□ arc

□ circuit

□ coil

□ cone

□ crescent

□ disk

□ flex

□ sphere

□ spiral

□ warp

303. Shapes (General Names)

Check (✔) the words you already know. Then, listen and repeat.

Tracks 1–3

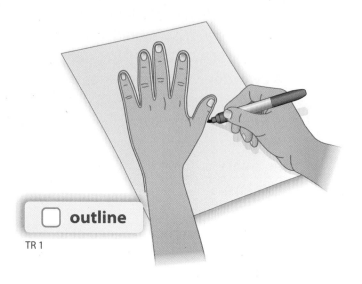

☐ **outline**

TR 1

☐ **pattern**

TR 2

Check Your Understanding

A. Choose the sentence that correctly uses the underlined word.

1. a. The <u>shape</u> rolled and rolled as it sailed in the rough seas.

   b. The young child drew the mountain in the <u>shape</u> of a triangle.

2. a. Greta baked the <u>outline</u> in the oven for twenty minutes.

   b. She drew an <u>outline</u> of her hand by placing it on the paper and tracing around her fingers.

3. a. I bought a scarf with a blue and green <u>pattern</u>.

   b. The audience listened to the lovely <u>pattern</u> of the woman singing.

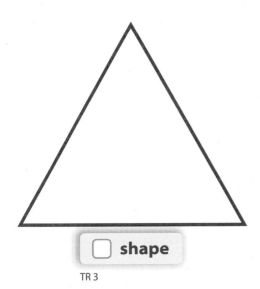

☐ **shape**

TR 3

Definitions

An **outline** of an object or person is its general shape.

A **pattern** is an arrangement of lines or shapes that form a design.

The **shape** of something is its form or outline.

B. Match each word to the correct description. One description will not be used.

1. _____ outline
2. _____ pattern
3. _____ shape

a. a shape that has two long sides and two short sides

b. the general shape of an object or person

c. the form of something

d. an arrangement of lines or shapes that form a design

Challenge Words

Check (✔) the words you already know.

☐ contour ☐ form ☐ oblong ☐ silhouette

☐ figure ☐ frame ☐ profile ☐ skyline

326. Bluntness / Sharpness

Check (✔) the words you already know. Then, listen and repeat.

Tracks 1–2

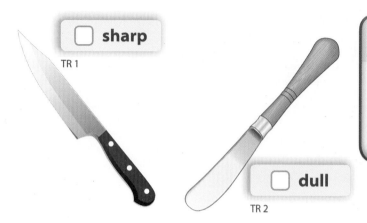

☐ **sharp**

TR 1

☐ **dull**

TR 2

Definitions

Something that is **dull** has a point or edge that is not sharp.

A **sharp** point or edge is very thin and can cut through things very easily.

Check Your Understanding

A. Underline the correct word to complete each sentence.

1. Louise accidentally cut her finger on the (**sharp / dull**) edge of the pocket knife.

2. The knife that Laura was using was so (**dull / sharp**) that it could not slice the tomato.

3. The scissors were (**dull / sharp**), so it was difficult to cut the paper neatly.

B. Choose the sentence that correctly uses the underlined word.

1. a. I laid my head on the <u>sharp</u> pillow and quickly fell asleep.

   b. Evan was careful when cleaning up the <u>sharp</u> pieces of the broken glass.

2. a. Marjorie bought herself a <u>dull</u>, crunchy apple.

   b. After many years, the clippers, saws, and other tools became <u>dull</u> and could no longer be used.

3. a. It hurt when the cat bit me with its <u>sharp</u> teeth.

   b. When I want to be comfortable, I put on my <u>sharp</u> wool socks.

Challenge Words

Check (✔) the words you already know.

☐ blunt   ☐ keen

42. Contractions (Are)

Check (✔) the words you already know. Then, listen and repeat.

Tracks 1–3

they + are = they're

☐ **they're**

TR 1

Definitions

They're is short for *they are.*

We're is short for *we are.*

You're is short for *you are.*

we + are = we're

☐ **we're**

TR 2

you + are = you're

☐ **you're**

TR 3

Check Your Understanding

A. Match each contraction to the correct long form. One long form will not be used.

1. _____ they're   a. you are

2. _____ you're   b. we are

3. _____ we're   c. where are

                       d. they are

B. Circle the correct word to complete each sentence.

1. I have to go to Bill's birthday party tomorrow night. _____ coming to the party with me, aren't you?

   a. They're   b. You're   c. We're

2. We bought four tickets to the concert. _____ going to sit in the first row!

   a. They're   b. You're   c. We're

3. Their car has a flat tire. _____ going to be late to the movie.

   a. They're   b. You're   c. We're

81. Contractions (Is)

Check (✔) the words you already know. Then, listen and repeat.

Tracks 1–9

he + is = he's

☐ he's

TR 1

I + am = I'm

☐ I'm

TR 2

it + is = it's

☐ it's

TR 3

she + is = she's

☐ she's

TR 4

that + is = that's

☐ that's

TR 6

there + is = there's

☐ there's

TR 8

Definitions

He's is short for *he is*.

Here's is short for *here is*.

I'm is short for *I am*.

It's is short for *it is*.

She's is short for *she is*.

That's is short for *that is*.

There's is short for *there is*.

What's is short for *what is*.

Where's is short for *where is*.

here + is = here's

☐ here's

TR 5

what + is = what's

☐ what's

TR 7

where + is = where's

☐ where's

TR 9

Check Your Understanding

A. Choose the correct word from the word bank to complete each sentence. One word will not be used. Capitalize words when necessary.

he's	I'm	she's	it's	that's
there's	here's	how's	what's	where's

1. Gloria is the best runner. I think _____ going to win the race.

2. _____ a gardener. I work all day in the garden.

3. _____ the remote control? I can't find it, and I want to watch television now.

4. _____ an angry boy. Look how red his face is.

5. _____ happening this weekend? We should make plans.

6. _____ time to go. It's 5:00, and the show starts at 5:45.

7. _____ a problem with the computer. It doesn't start.

8. We did the calculation. We are sure _____ the correct answer.

9. _____ my passport. Could you put it in your pocket and hold it for me?

B. Underline the correct word to complete each sentence.

1. (**That's / I'll**) the best one.

2. (**Where's / There's**) a note for you on the table.

3. My throat is sore. I think (**there's / I'm**) sick.

4. (**Where's / I'm**) Timmy? He's always late.

5. Mr. Smith teaches math. (**What's / He's**) my favorite teacher.

6. With the blowing wind, (**where's / it's**) really cold outside.

7. (**He's / Here's**) a cup of hot tea. I think it will help you feel better.

8. (**I'm / What's**) important is that no one was hurt in the accident.

9. I love my mom's food. (**She's / It's**) a great cook.

Challenge Words

Check (✔) the word if you already know it.

☐ how's

85. Contractions (Will)

Check (✔) the words you already know. Then, listen and repeat.

Tracks 1–6

he + will = he'll

☐ **he'll**

TR 1

I + will = I'll

☐ **I'll**

TR 2

she + will = she'll

☐ **she'll**

TR 3

we + will = we'll

☐ **we'll**

TR 5

Definitions

He'll is short for *he will.*

I'll is short for *I will.*

She'll is short for *she will.*

They'll is short for *they will.*

We'll is short for *we will.*

You'll is short for *you will.*

they + will = they'll

☐ **they'll**

TR 4

you + will = you'll

☐ **you'll**

TR 6

Check Your Understanding

A. Underline the correct word to complete each sentence.

1. Could you pick up Becky from the airport? (**She'll / I'll**) be the girl wearing the blue dress.

2. I have to leave now or (**you'll / I'll**) miss my bus.

3. John said that (**he'll / they'll**) lend me his car for the weekend.

4. (**They'll / I'll**) scare all the fish away if they make too much noise.

5. Julia and I are going on vacation. (**We'll / They'll**) be visiting Julia's family for two weeks.

6. If you don't eat now, (**you'll / he'll**) be hungry later.

B. Match each contraction to the correct long form. Two long forms will not be used.

1. _____ she'll   a. you will

2. _____ I'll   b. there will

3. _____ he'll   c. they will

4. _____ we'll   d. she will

5. _____ you'll   e. I will

6. _____ they'll   f. he will

     g. we will

     h. what will

Challenge Words

Check (✔) the words you already know.

☐ there'll   ☐ what'll

150. Contractions (Have)

Check (✔) the words you already know. Then, listen and repeat.

Tracks 1–4

I + have = I've

☐ **I've**

TR 1

they + have = they've

☐ **they've**

TR 2

we + have = we've

☐ **we've**

TR 3

you + have = you've

☐ **you've**

TR 4

Definitions

I've is short for *I have.*

They've is short for *they have,* especially when *have* is an auxiliary verb.

We've is short for *we have.*

You've is short for *you have.*

Check Your Understanding

A. Underline the correct word to complete each sentence.

1. (**I've** / **They've**) become our friends.

2. (**You've** / **I've**) seen a blue whale with my own eyes.

3. (**They've** / **We've**) never been to this beach before, but they have.

4. (**You've** / **We've**) got to pay for your own ticket because I don't have any money left.

B. Choose the correct word from the word bank to complete each sentence. One word will not be used.

we're	you've	I've
we've	they've	

1. The winning ticket is mine. _____ won the prize!

2. It is really late for you. _____ got to go home now.

3. _____ had a great time. Our vacation was a success.

4. My grandparents love the ocean, so _____ decided to buy a house near

   the beach.

235. Contractions (Not)

Check (✔) the words you already know. Then, listen and repeat.

Tracks 1–13

do + not = don't

☐ don't

TR 1

can + not = can't

☐ can't

TR 2

is + not = isn't

☐ isn't

TR 3

has + not = hasn't

☐ hasn't

TR 4

am + not
are + not
is + not   = ain't
has + not
have + not

☐ ain't

TR 5

could + not = couldn't

☐ couldn't

TR 6

have + not = haven't

☐ haven't

TR 8

are + not = aren't

☐ aren't

TR 7

should + not = shouldn't

☐ shouldn't

TR 10

does + not = doesn't

☐ doesn't

TR 9

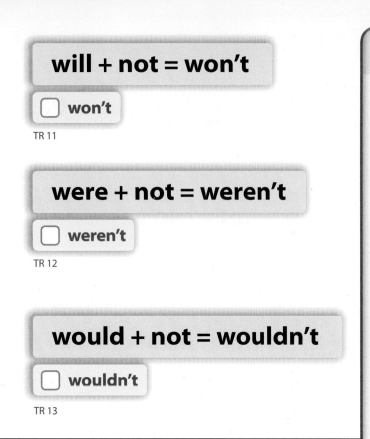

will + not = won't

☐ won't

TR 11

were + not = weren't

☐ weren't

TR 12

would + not = wouldn't

☐ wouldn't

TR 13

Definitions

Ain't is short for *am not, are not, is not, have not,* and *has not.* Many people think that *ain't* is grammatically incorrect.

Aren't is short for *are not.*

Can't is short for *cannot.*

Couldn't is short for *could not.*

Doesn't is short for *does not.*

Don't is short for *do not.*

Hasn't is short for *has not.*

Haven't is short for *have not.*

Isn't is short for *is not.*

Shouldn't is short for *should not.*

Weren't is short for *were not.*

Won't is short for *will not.*

Wouldn't is short for *would not.*

Check Your Understanding

A. Match each contraction to the correct long form. Two long forms will not be used.

1. _____ couldn't   a. would not
2. _____ isn't   b. are not
3. _____ don't   c. will not
4. _____ wouldn't   d. cannot
5. _____ weren't   e. was not
6. _____ haven't   f. could not
7. _____ doesn't   g. have not
8. _____ can't   h. has not
9. _____ aren't   i. must not
10. _____ won't   j. am not and are not
11. _____ shouldn't   k. do not
12. _____ hasn't   l. is not
13. _____ ain't   m. does not

n. should not

o. were not

B. Choose the sentence that correctly uses the underlined word.

1. a. I <u>wouldn't</u> want to be in that situation.

   b. They were very hungry, so they <u>wouldn't</u> eat.

2. a. They <u>weren't</u> the ones we wanted.

   b. I <u>weren't</u> a student.

3. a. He <u>haven't</u> been to the park in five days.

   b. Jen and Franny <u>haven't</u> had a cup of coffee in two days.

4. a. They <u>doesn't</u> eat seafood.

   b. He <u>doesn't</u> know where she lives.

5. a. It's so cold. I <u>can't</u> feel my fingers.

   b. We <u>can't</u> going to the movies tonight.

6. a. There <u>aren't</u> a painting in my living room.

   b. These <u>aren't</u> the right color.

7. a. We <u>couldn't</u> see over the fence.

   b. Selena <u>couldn't</u> worried about the test.

8. a. These <u>won't</u> my socks.

   b. She <u>won't</u> listen to me.

9. a. I <u>hasn't</u> scored a point in this game.

   b. She <u>hasn't</u> taken her medicine yet.

10. a. They <u>shouldn't</u> drive tonight.

    b. <u>Shouldn't</u> she coming with us?

11. a. That red cat <u>don't</u> lives in the blue house.

    b. We <u>don't</u> know how to get to the mall.

12. a. This <u>isn't</u> my cell phone.

    b. I <u>isn't</u> sure how much it costs.

13. a. We <u>ain't</u> going to follow that person.

    b. Devon <u>ain't</u> his way to the bakery.

Challenge Words

Check (✔) the words you already know.

☐ hadn't   ☐ musn't   ☐ wasn't

274. Contractions (Would)

Check (✔) the words you already know. Then, listen and repeat.

Tracks 1–5

he + would = he'd

☐ he'd

TR 1

she + would = she'd

☐ she'd

TR 3

I + would = I'd

☐ I'd

TR 2

Check Your Understanding

A. Choose the correct word from the word bank to complete each sentence. One word will not be used.

I'd	he'd	she'd
we'd	they'd	you'd

1. Can you help me please? _____ like to try on that ring.

2. My brothers said that _____ come to the party if they had time.

3. Ava decided that _____ take the job because she needed money.

4. I know that _____ help me if you could.

5. John said that _____ go to the beach with me tomorrow.

they + would = they'd

☐ **they'd**

TR 4

you + would = you'd

☐ **you'd**

TR 5

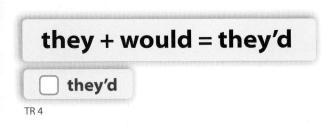

Definitions

He'd is short for *he would.*

I'd is short for *I would.*

She'd is short for *she would.*

They'd is short for *they would.*

You'd is short for *you would.*

B. Underline the correct word to complete each sentence.

1. I think (**you'd / I'd**) be a good basketball player because you are very tall.

2. If the kids stayed in the sun all day, (**you'd / they'd**) probably be hot and tired.

3. (**She'd / They'd**) get a lot of votes for class president because she has so many friends.

4. I am so tired. (**He'd / I'd**) like to go to sleep right now.

5. (**He'd / You'd**) better get ready to go because his school bus is about the arrive at his house.

56. People (General Names)

Check (✔) the words you already know. Then, listen and repeat.

Tracks 1–6

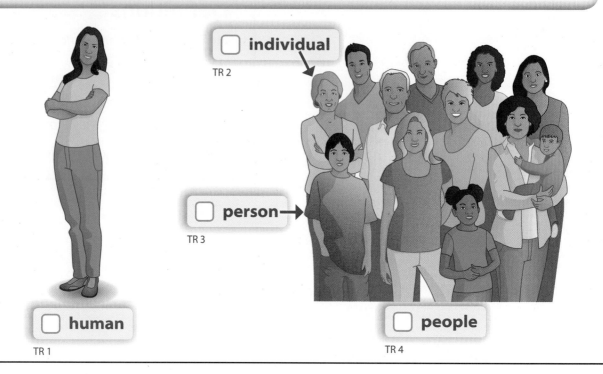

☐ individual

TR 2

☐ person

TR 3

☐ human

TR 1

☐ people

TR 4

Check Your Understanding

A. Circle the correct word to complete each sentence.

1. Four _____ were selected to go to New York this summer.

   a. selves   b. peoples   c. individuals

2. How many _____ are coming to the party?

   a. people   b. self   c. person

3. Rosa showed her best _____ at the competition today. She was very positive and did well.

   a. individual   b. people   c. self

4. Fido is not a name for a _____. It's a name for a dog.

   a. hero   b. human   c. people

5. Jon is a very nice _____.

   a. people   b. person   c. self

6. My dad has done so many good deeds. He really is my _____.

   a. human   b. individual   c. hero

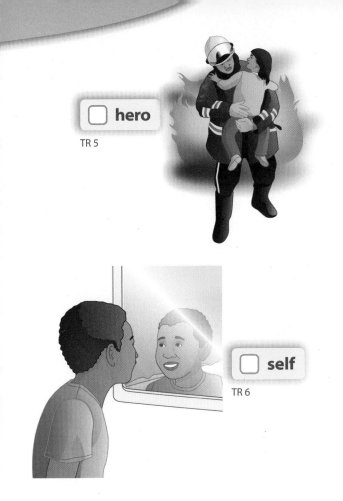

hero

TR 5

self

TR 6

Definitions

A **hero** is someone who does something brave or good.

A **human** is a person, rather than an animal or a machine.

An **individual** is one person.

People are men, women, and children.

A **person** is a single human being—a man, woman, or child.

Your **self** is your own personality or nature.

B. Underline the correct word to complete each sentence.

1. A/An (**individual / humans**) from my class was chosen to visit Japan.

2. Thirty-five (**selfs / people**) came to the picnic last Saturday.

3. In science class, we look at pictures of (**humans / heroes**) and animals to understand how their bodies work.

4. Who is that (**people / person**) sitting in your car?

5. Who is your (**hero / human**)?

6. You look much happier today than you did yesterday. You look like your old (**self / individual**) again.

Challenge Words

Check (✔) the words you already know.

- [ ] being
- [ ] character
- [ ] folk
- [ ] heroine
- [ ] highness
- [ ] mankind

94. Family Relationships

Check (✔) the words you already know. Then, listen and repeat.

Tracks 1–23

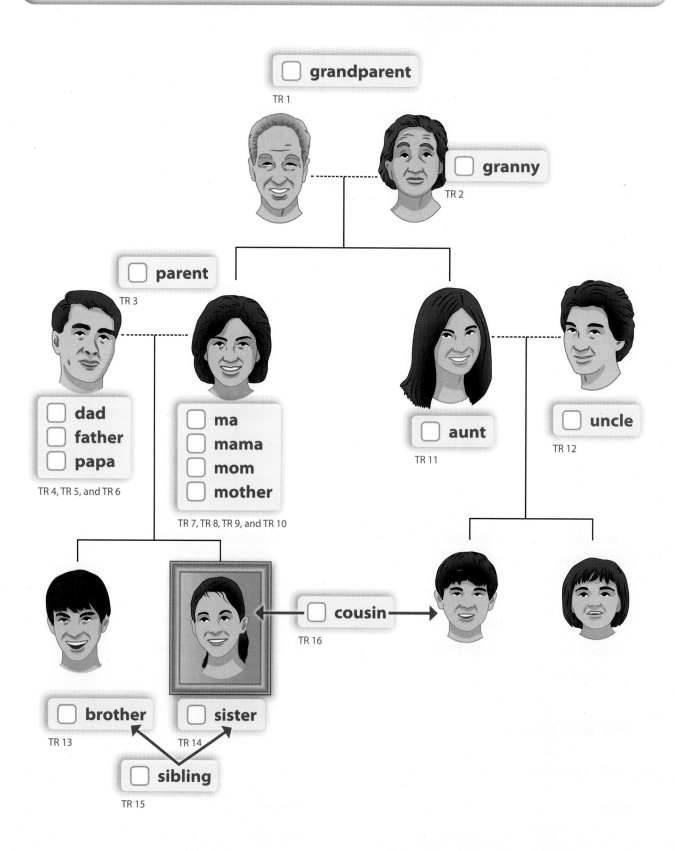

☐ **grandparent**

TR 1

☐ **granny**

TR 2

☐ **parent**

TR 3

☐ **dad**
☐ **father**
☐ **papa**

TR 4, TR 5, and TR 6

☐ **ma**
☐ **mama**
☐ **mom**
☐ **mother**

TR 7, TR 8, TR 9, and TR 10

☐ **aunt**

TR 11

☐ **uncle**

TR 12

☐ **cousin**

TR 16

☐ **brother**

TR 13

☐ **sister**

TR 14

☐ **sibling**

TR 15

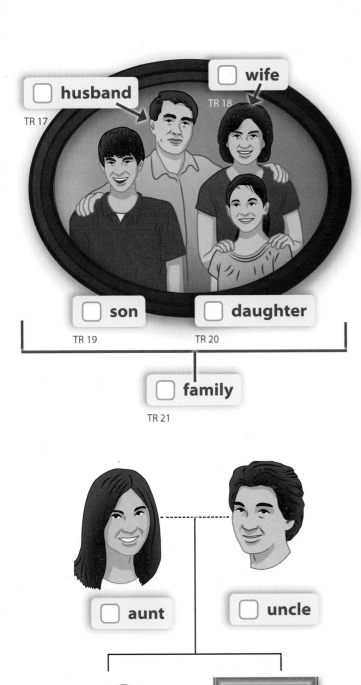

Definitions

Your **aunt** is the sister of your mother or father, or the wife of your uncle.

Your **brother** is a boy or a man who has the same parents as you.

Your **cousin** is the child of your uncle or aunt.

Your **dad** is your father.

Someone's **daughter** is that person's female child.

A **family** is a group of people who are related to each other, and usually includes parents and their children.

Your **father** is your male parent.

Your **grandparents** are the parents of your father or mother.

Granny is an informal word for *grandmother*.

A woman's **husband** is the man she is married to.

Ma means the same as *mother*.

Mama means the same as *mother*.

Your **mom** is your mother.

Your **mother** is your female parent.

Your **nephew** is the son of your sister or brother.

Your **niece** is the daughter of your sister or brother.

Papa means the same as *father*.

Your **parents** are your mother and your father.

Your **siblings** are your brothers and sisters.

Your **sister** is a girl or a woman who has the same parents as you.

Someone's **son** is that person's male child.

Your **uncle** is the brother of your mother or father, or the husband of your aunt.

A man's **wife** is the woman he is married to.

Check Your Understanding

A. Match each word to the correct description. Some descriptions will have more than one answer. One word will not be used.

1. _____ the woman that a man marries
2. _____ your father's sister
3. _____ another name for *grandmother*
4. _____ your mom and your dad
5. _____ your female parent
6. _____ your brother's daughter
7. _____ group of people that are related to you
8. _____ the man that a woman marries
9. _____ your brother or sister
10. _____ the children of your aunt and uncle
11. _____ your father's brother
12. _____ your grandfather or grandmother
13. _____ your male parent
14. _____ your male sibling
15. _____ a female child
16. _____ your female sibling
17. _____ a male child
18. _____ your sibling's son

a. cousins
b. uncle
c. son
d. sister
e. husband
f. family
g. mama
h. father
i. dad
j. ma
k. maternal
l. brother
m. sibling
n. wife
o. aunt
p. grandparents
q. mother
r. papa
s. niece
t. mom
u. daughter
v. parents
w. granny
x. nephew

B. Underline the correct word(s) to complete each sentence.

1. The parents of your mother and father are your (**grandparents / cousins**).

2. Another name for your mother is (**granny / mom**) or (**sibling / ma**).

3. Your aunt's children are your (**cousins / nieces**).

4. When a man marries a woman, she becomes his (**aunt / wife**).

5. If your aunt gets married, her husband is your (**papa / uncle**).

6. A child might call her grandmother (**mama / granny**).

7. Your male cousin is your mother's (**nephew / brother**) and your female cousin is your mother's (**sister / niece**).

8. Your male sibling is your (**brother / uncle**).

9. Your male parent is your (**ma / father**).

10. Your mother, father, and siblings make up your (**grandparents / family**).

11. If your uncle gets married, his wife is your (**aunt / parent**).

12. A young child might call his mother (**family / mama**).

13. Your brothers and sisters are your (**siblings / sons**).

14. The man that a woman marries becomes her (**husband / nephew**).

15. Your female parent is your (**aunt / mother**).

16. Your female sibling is your (**family / sister**).

17. You might call your father (**son / dad**) or (**papa / brother**).

18. A female child is her parents' (**daughter / granny**).

19. Your mother and father are your (**parents** / **grandparents**).

20. A male child is his parents' (**papa** / **son**).

Challenge Words

Check (✔) the words you already know.

☐ ancestor   ☐ groom   ☐ household   ☐ patriarch

☐ bride   ☐ guardian   ☐ maternal   ☐ spouse

111. Females

Check (✔) the words you already know. Then, listen and repeat.

Tracks 1–6

☐ **girl**

TR 1

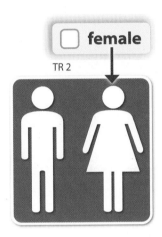

☐ **female**

TR 2

Definitions

A **female** is a woman or a girl.

A **girl** is a female child.

A **housewife** is a woman who spends most of her time at home looking after her house and family.

You can use the word **lady** when you are talking about a woman in a polite way.

A **schoolgirl** is a female child who attends school.

A **woman** is an adult female.

☐ **housewife**

TR 3

☐ **lady**
☐ **woman**

TR 4 and TR 5

☐ **schoolgirl**

TR 6

Check Your Understanding

A. Write **T** for **true statements** and **F** for **false statements**.

1. _____ A girl is an adult female.

2. _____ The word *female* can refer to an adult or a child.

3. _____ A schoolgirl stays home all day and cares for the house.

4. _____ A housewife takes care of her family.

5. _____ A woman is an adult female.

6. _____ The word *lady* is an impolite way to talk about a woman.

B. Choose the correct description for each word.

1. girl

   a. young female   b. a person who goes to school

2. lady

   a. a mother   b. a polite word for *woman*

3. woman

   a. a female child   b. a female adult

4. female

   a. a young person   b. a girl or a woman

5. housewife

   a. a woman who takes care   b. a woman who goes to school
      of her home and family

6. schoolgirl

   a. a polite word for *girl*   b. a girl who goes to school

Challenge Words

Check (✔) the words you already know.

☐ belle   ☐ hostess   ☐ madam   ☐ tomboy

☐ dame   ☐ lass   ☐ spinster   ☐ widow

203. Males

Check (✔) the words you already know. Then, listen and repeat.

 Tracks 1–6

☐ **boy**

TR 1

☐ **guy**
☐ **man**

TR 2 and TR 3

Definitions

A **boy** is a male child.

Guy is an informal word for *man*.

A **male** is a person that belongs to the sex that does not have babies.

A **man** is an adult male human.

A **schoolboy** is a male child who attends school.

You use **sir** as a polite way of talking to a man.

Excuse me, **sir!**

☐ **sir**

TR 4

☐ **schoolboy**

TR 5

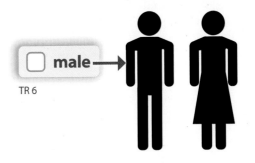

☐ **male** →

TR 6

245

Check Your Understanding

A. Choose the correct word from the word bank to answer each question. One word will not be used.

males	boy	sir	man
schoolboys	guy	junior	

1. What people cannot have babies? _____

2. Which word do you use to be polite to a man? _____

3. What is a male child called? _____

4. Which word can also mean *man?* _____

5. When a boy becomes an adult, what is he? _____

6. What word describes young males in school? _____

B. Underline the correct word to complete each sentence.

1. Who is the new (**guy / sir**)? I have never seen him before.

2. William is a serious (**male / man**) that never smiles.

3. The (**sirs / schoolboys**) lined up to get on the bus.

4. Pardon me, (**sir / guy**), but do you know what time it is?

5. A boy and a man are both (**schoolboys / males**).

6. A four-year-old (**man / boy**) lives in the house next door.

Challenge Words

Check (✔) the words you already know.

☐ bachelor ☐ fellow ☐ junior ☐ masculine

☐ dude ☐ host ☐ lad ☐ mister

204. Names that Indicate Age

Check (✔) the words you already know. Then, listen and repeat.

 Tracks 1–7

☐ **baby**

TR 1

☐ **toddler**

TR 2

Definitions

An **adult** is a fully grown person.

A **baby** is a very young child.

A **child** is a young boy or girl.

Grown-up is a word for an adult.

Kid is an informal word used for a child.

A **teenager** is someone who is between thirteen and nineteen years old.

A **toddler** is a young child who has only just learned to walk.

☐ **child**
☐ **kid**

TR 3 and TR 4

☐ **adult**
☐ **grown-up**

TR 6 and TR 7

☐ **teenager**

TR 5

247

Check Your Understanding

A. Underline the correct word to complete each sentence.

1. The preschool teacher explained to the class that a (**baby / grown-up**) has to help them cut out shapes.

2. All the little (**babies / adults**) were sleeping in the hospital's nursery.

3. Michael is now a (**teenager / child**). He is celebrating his thirteenth birthday today!

4. There will be fifteen (**adults / kids**) at the party. I hope that there are enough adults to watch them.

5. Now that Elisa is two, she can go to the playgroup with the other (**toddlers / grown-ups**).

6. Eric cannot drive a car because he is a (**grown-up / child**).

7. The wedding invitation says that (**kids / adults**) can come, but not children.

B. Write the words from the word bank on the line in order from **youngest** to **oldest**.

child	baby	teenager	kid
adult	toddler	grown-up	

1. _____

2. _____

3. _____ or _____

4. _____

5. _____ or _____

Challenge Words

Check (✔) the words you already know.

☐ elder ☐ juvenile ☐ newborn ☐ tot

☐ infant ☐ minor ☐ senior ☐ youngster

248

205. Names that Indicate Camaraderie / Friendship

Check (✔) the words you already know. Then, listen and repeat.

Tracks 1–7

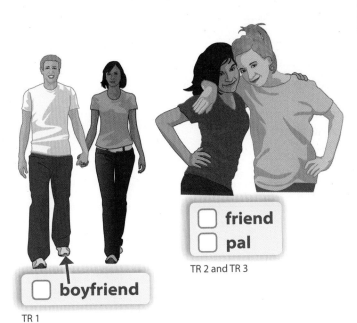

☐ **friend**
☐ **pal**

TR 2 and TR 3

☐ **boyfriend**

TR 1

Definitions

A **boyfriend** of a woman or a girl is a man or a boy that she is having a romantic relationship with.

A **classmate** is a student who is in the same class as you at school.

A **friend** is someone who you like and know well.

Your **neighbor** is someone who lives near you.

Pal is an informal word for *friend*.

Your **partner** is your husband or wife, or your boyfriend or girlfriend.

A child's **playmate** is another child who plays with them.

☐ **classmate**

TR 4

☐ **neighbor**

TR 5

☐ **partner**

TR 6

☐ **playmate**

TR 7

Check Your Understanding

A. Choose the best word from the word bank to answer the questions below. One word will not be used.

| boyfriend | friend | pal | partner |
| acquaintance | classmates | neighbor | playmates |

1. Who are the people that attend the same classes as you? _____
2. With whom does a child share her toys? _____
3. What is another word for *friend*? _____
4. What do you call a man who has a romantic relationship with a woman but is not married to her? _____
5. What do you call a person that you really like but who is not part of your family? _____
6. Who lives in the house next to yours? _____
7. What is another way to say *husband* or *wife*? _____

B. Circle the correct word to complete each sentence.

1. All the _____ that live on our street are very helpful.
   a. partners   b. boyfriends   c. neighbors
2. Did you know that Carlos is Jenny's _____? They have been dating for three months.
   a. classmate   b. boyfriend   c. pal
3. Since all the children were _____, their mothers became friends.
   a. partners   b. playmates   c. boyfriends
4. Some of Rob's _____ are going to help him move to a new apartment.
   a. playmates   b. partners   c. pals
5. Susana is so popular! She has many _____.
   a. friends   b. neighbors   c. classmates
6. My mother thinks that it's important for adults to have a _____ for life.
   a. classmate   b. partner   c. playmate
7. When he got to school, Martin realized he forgot a pen, so he asked a _____ if he could borrow one.
   a. neighbor   b. playmate   c. classmate

Challenge Words

Check (✔) the words you already know.

☐ acquaintance   ☐ companion   ☐ mate   ☐ sweetheart
☐ buddy   ☐ fiancé (fiancée)   ☐ peer   ☐ teammate

206. Names that Indicate Negative Characteristics About People

Check (✔) the words you already know. Then, listen and repeat.

Tracks 1–9

☐ **bandit**

TR 1

☐ **enemy**

TR 2

☐ **thief**

TR 3

WANTED
FOR ROBBERY

Anyone with information is asked to call the FBI office or law enforcement agency.
DANGEROUS

☐ **criminal**

TR 4

Definitions

A **bandit** is a person who robs people who are traveling.

A **bully** is someone who uses their strength or power to frighten other people.

A **criminal** is a person who commits a serious crime.

If someone is your **enemy**, they dislike you and might want to harm you.

A **killer** is someone who has killed another person.

A **liar** is someone who tells lies.

A **pirate** is a person who attacks ships and steals property from others.

A **thief** is a person who steals something from another person.

A **villain** is someone in a movie or story who deliberately harms other people or breaks the law.

WORLD POST
KILLER CONVICTED

☐ **killer**

TR 5

☐ **bully**

TR 6

I got an A on the test.

☐ **liar**

TR 9

EYEWITNESS NEWS

PIRATES CAPTURE SHIP

☐ **villain**

TR 8

☐ **pirate**

TR 7

Check Your Understanding

A. Match each word to the correct description. One description will not be used.

1. _____ bully
2. _____ pirate
3. _____ bandit
4. _____ criminal
5. _____ liar
6. _____ killer
7. _____ enemy
8. _____ villain
9. _____ thief

a. a stupid or silly person

b. somebody who steals things from other people

c. someone who does not tell the truth

d. a person who uses strength to frighten others

e. a person who dislikes you

f. a criminal who steals from people while they are traveling

g. a criminal who works on the ocean

h. someone in a movie who intentionally harms others

i. a person who has taken another person's life

j. anybody who commits a serious crime

B. Write **T** for **true statements** and **F** for **false statements**.

1. _____ A bandit travels the ocean looking for ships to rob.

2. _____ Many movies have villains that cause problems for the hero of the movie.

3. _____ A bully is a person who tries to fight with or frighten other people.

4. _____ A thief is an example of a criminal.

5. _____ You would probably like to take a vacation with your enemies.

6. _____ Killers do not harm people.

7. _____ People really like to be with liars because they know they can be trusted.

8. _____ A pirate is a robber who takes things from people on boats.

9. _____ If your classmate has money sticking out of his pocket and you take it, you are a thief.

Challenge Words

Check (✔) the words you already know.

☐ burglar ☐ fool ☐ moron ☐ opponent ☐ rival

☐ delinquent ☐ gossip ☐ nuisance ☐ pest ☐ snob

227. Names for Spiritual / Mythological Characters

Check (✔) the words you already know. Then, listen and repeat.

 Tracks 1–10

☐ **angel**
TR 1

☐ **elf**
TR 2

☐ **god**
TR 3

☐ **ghost**
TR 4

☐ **wizard**
TR 6

☐ **witch**
TR 5

Definitions

An **angel** is a spiritual being that some people believe exist.

A **cupid** is a winged boy with a bow and arrow that represents love.

Some people believe that the **devil** is an evil spirit that makes bad things happen.

An **elf** is a small, sneaky, imaginary person in folktales.

A **fairy** is a very small, winged creature that has magical powers.

A **ghost** is the spirit of a dead person.

In many cultures, a **god** is a spirit that has a power over a particular part of the world or nature.

In stories, a **monster** is a scary, imaginary creature.

In children's stories, a **witch** is a woman who has magical powers.

In children's stories, a **wizard** is a man who has magical powers.

☐ **devil**
TR 7

☐ **fairy**
TR 8

☐ **cupid**
TR 9

☐ **monster**
TR 10

Check Your Understanding

A. Choose the word or phrase that correctly completes each sentence.

1. A ghost is a (**woman with magical powers / dead person's spirit**).

2. A god is a (**dead person's spirit / being with special powers**).

3. A witch is a (**woman with magical powers / small creature with wings**).

4. A monster is a (**small, winged / scary**) creature.

5. A wizard is a (**man with magical powers / large, furry creature that lives in the forest**).

6. A fairy is a (**small creature with magical powers / dead person's spirit**).

7. An angel is (**a spiritual being / an evil spirit**).

8. A devil is (**a woman who has wings / an evil spirit that makes bad things happen**).

9. A cupid is (**a boy / an old woman**) who represents romance.

10. An elf is a (**large, imaginary person who flies / a small, imaginary person who plays tricks on others**).

B. Write **T** for **true statements** and **F** for **false statements**.

1. _____ Some people believe that the devil is an evil being.

2. _____ A wizard is the spirit of someone who has died.

3. _____ Fairies are not real.

4. _____ An angel is a very small, evil person that lives in the forest.

5. _____ An elf is a very small girl that is able to fly.

6. _____ Cupid is often associated with romance and love.

7. _____ A ghost is the same thing as a living person.

8. _____ A witch uses magic.

9. _____ Monsters are imaginary creatures that children may read about in stories.

10. _____ All people believe in a god.

Challenge Words

Check (✔) the words you already know.

- ☐ deity
- ☐ genie
- ☐ goblin
- ☐ phantom
- ☐ saint
- ☐ soul
- ☐ vampire
- ☐ werewolf

317. Lack of Permanence (People)

Check (✔) the words you already know. Then, listen and repeat.

Tracks 1–3

HAPPY BIRTHDAY!

☐ **guest**

TR 1

Definitions

A **guest** is someone who is invited to your home or to an event.

A **stranger** is someone that you have never met before.

A **visitor** is someone who is visiting a person or a place.

☐ **stranger**

TR 2

☐ **visitor**

TR 3

Check Your Understanding

A. Underline the correct word to complete each sentence.

1. I got lost on my way to the park, so I asked a (**visitor / stranger**) for directions.

2. Grandma will be a (**guest / stranger**) in our house for the next two weeks.

3. How many (**guests / visitors**) does the White House attract each year?

B. Choose the correct word from the word bank to complete each sentence. One word will not be used.

stranger	passenger	visitor	guest

1. When you go to a museum or a monument, you are a _____ .

2. When you go to a wedding, you are a _____ .

3. When you move to a new city where you do not know anyone, you are a

_____ .

Challenge Words

Check (✔) the words you already know.

- ☐ migrant
- ☐ spectator
- ☐ vacationer
- ☐ passenger
- ☐ tourist
- ☐ wanderer

32 CATEGORIES OF PEOPLE

330. Size of People

Check (✔) the words you already know. Then, listen and repeat.

Tracks 1–2

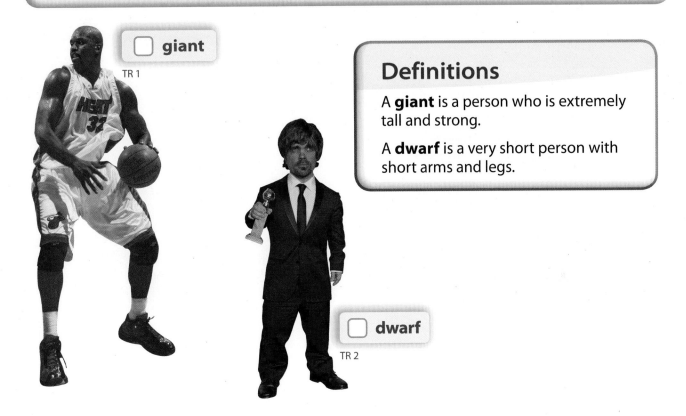

☐ **giant**
TR 1

☐ **dwarf**
TR 2

Definitions

A **giant** is a person who is extremely tall and strong.

A **dwarf** is a very short person with short arms and legs.

Check Your Understanding

A. Write **T** for **true statements** and **F** for **false statements**.

1. _____ Giants are very short.
2. _____ Dwarfs have long arms and long legs.
3. _____ Giants have powerful bodies.
4. _____ A dwarf is not tall.

B. Choose the correct word from the word bank to complete each sentence. One word will be used two times.

> giant   dwarf

1. An adult who is less than four feet tall may be a _____.
2. Someone who is a _____ has clothing made especially for him because the clothes sold at stores are too small.
3. A _____ has short arms and short legs.

257

343. Names that Indicate Permanence for People

Check (✔) the words you already know. Then, listen and repeat.

Tracks 1–3

☐ **caveman**

TR 1

☐ **citizen**

TR 2

Check Your Understanding

A. Choose the correct word from the word bank to complete each sentence. One word will not be used.

pioneers	citizen	taxpayers	cavemen

1. In ancient times, _____ would hunt food and use fire to cook it.

2. Maurice is going to become a _____ of this country tomorrow.

3. _____ had to make difficult decisions when choosing to leave their homelands.

Definitions

A **caveman** is a human who lived long ago.

A **citizen** is someone who legally belongs to a particular country, state, or city.

A **pioneer** is one of the first people to enter new or undeveloped land to live and work there.

☐ **pioneer**

TR 3

B. Underline the correct word to complete each sentence.

1. Many (**citizens / pioneers**) traveled to new places in covered wagons.

2. Most (**cavemen / pioneers**) lived in caves and made tools to hunt for their food.

3. I was born in New York, so I am a (**caveman / citizen**) of the United States.

Challenge Words

Check (✔) the words you already know.

☐ alien   ☐ newcomer   ☐ taxpayer   ☐ townspeople

☐ native   ☐ pilgrim   ☐ tenant   ☐ villager

344. Names that Indicate Fame

Check (✔) the words you already know. Then, listen and repeat.

Tracks 1–2

- [ ] **celebrity**
- [ ] **star**

TR 1 and TR 2

Definitions

A **celebrity** is somebody who is famous.

A **star** is a famous actor, musician, or sports player.

Check Your Understanding

A. Write **T** for **true statements** and **F** for **false statements**.

1. _____ Celebrities are famous.

2. _____ A star is someone who works for the government.

3. _____ Celebrities are famous, but stars are not.

4. _____ A star is someone who is careful.

B. Choose the correct word from the word bank to complete each sentence. Words may be used more than once. One word will not be used.

savior	star	celebrity

1. Anita was the _____ of the play. She had the main part.

2. The television weatherman is an example of a local _____ .

3. Everybody in town knew when Luke won the lottery. He became a _____ .

4. The high school football _____ went on to play football professionally.

Challenge Words

Check (✔) the words you already know.

- [ ] idol
- [ ] savior

382. Experience / Expertise

Check (✔) the words you already know. Then, listen and repeat.

 Tracks 1–2

beginner

TR 1

☐ expert

TR 2

Definitions

A **beginner** is someone who has just started learning to do something.

An **expert** is a person who knows a lot about something.

Check Your Understanding

A. Choose the sentence that correctly uses the underlined word.

1. a. In language classes, the <u>beginners</u> never make mistakes.

   b. Lisa had never skied before, so she took a lesson for <u>beginners</u>.

2. a. My aunt wrote a cookbook because she is an <u>expert</u> at cooking.

   b. He is an <u>expert</u> about cars, so he knows very little about them.

3. a. Melinda is an <u>expert</u> at solving arguments between her brothers. When she is around, there is no arguing.

   b. I don't know how to ride horses because I am an <u>expert</u>.

B. Write **T** for **true statements** and **F** for **false statements**.

1. _____ A science teacher is a beginner at science.

2. _____ To become an expert musician, you have to practice a lot.

3. _____ First-graders are expert readers.

4. _____ If you have studied English for many years, you are probably a beginner.

Challenge Words

Check (✔) the words you already know.

☐ ace   ☐ genius   ☐ pro   ☐ specialist

☐ amateur   ☐ novice   ☐ scholar   ☐ veteran

50. Bodies in Space

Check (✔) the words you already know. Then, listen and repeat.

Tracks 1–9

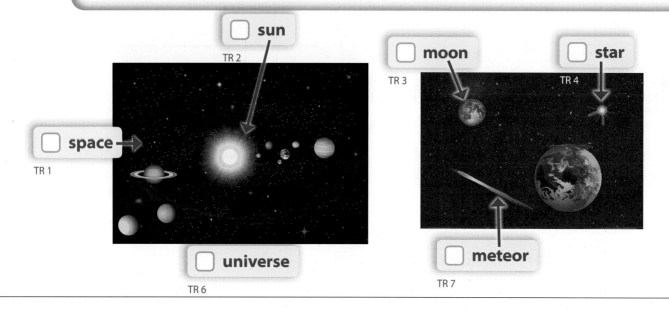

☐ sun
TR 2

☐ moon
TR 3

☐ star
TR 4

☐ space
TR 1

☐ universe
TR 6

☐ meteor
TR 7

Check Your Understanding

A. Match each word to the correct description. One description will not be used.

1. _____ moon
2. _____ sky
3. _____ star
4. _____ sun
5. _____ universe
6. _____ world
7. _____ meteor
8. _____ planet
9. _____ space

a. made up of stars, planets, and moons and is so big that it cannot be measured
b. another name for the Earth
c. a large object that moves around the Earth and shines in the sky at night
d. a bright, hot ball of gas that is seen at night
e. where airplanes and birds fly
f. where a rocket ship flies to
g. an object that starts to burn when it comes into the Earth's atmosphere
h. the large star that provides the Earth with heat and light
i. a large, round object that moves around an object—Earth is an example
j. a bright object with a tail that travels around the sun

B. Choose the sentence that correctly uses the underlined word.

1. a. The <u>moon</u> is an object with a tail that moves around the sun.
   b. The <u>moon</u> moves around the Earth.

2. a. On a rainy day, the <u>sky</u> is cloudy and gray.
   b. When I go outside and look down, I see the <u>sky</u>.

3. a. A <u>star</u> is a large moon that burns in space.
   b. A <u>star</u> is a burning ball of gas that gives off light.

□ sky

TR 5

□ planet

TR 8

□ world

TR 9

Definitions

A **meteor** is a small body of matter from space that burns very brightly when it enters the Earth's atmosphere.

The **moon** is the large, round object that moves around Earth. You can see the moon shining in the sky at night as it reflects light from the sun.

A **planet** is a large body that is shaped like a ball and moves around an object in outer space. Earth is a planet.

The **sky** is the area above the Earth that you can see when you stand outside and look upward.

Space is the area beyond the Earth's atmosphere where the stars and planets are.

A **star** is a bright, hot ball of gas in space. At night, stars look like small dots of light in the sky.

The **sun** is the the star around which the Earth and other planets revolve. The sun gives Earth light, heat, and energy.

The **universe** is everything that exists in space, including the Earth, the sun, the moon, the planets, and the stars.

The **world** is the planet that we live on.

4. a. The <u>sun</u> moves around the planets.

   b. The <u>sun</u> is a star.

5. a. Stars, moons, and planets exist in the <u>universe</u>.

   b. The <u>universe</u> is made up of only moons and meteors.

6. a. The <u>world</u> is where we live.

   b. The <u>world</u> burns when it enters the Earth's atmosphere.

7. a. A <u>meteor</u> is a small body of matter from space that burns brightly.

   b. You can see clouds and the sun when you look at a <u>meteor</u>.

8. a. The sun is a <u>planet</u>.

   b. The Earth is a <u>planet</u>.

9. a. When something goes outside of the Earth's atmosphere, it enters <u>space</u>.

   b. When something goes into the sky, it enters <u>space</u>.

Challenge Words

Check (✔) the words you already know.

□ asteroid   □ comet   □ eclipse   □ globe   □ satellite

□ celestial   □ constellation   □ galaxy   □ lunar   □ solar

114. Areas of Land

Check (✔) the words you already know. Then, listen and repeat.

Tracks 1–8

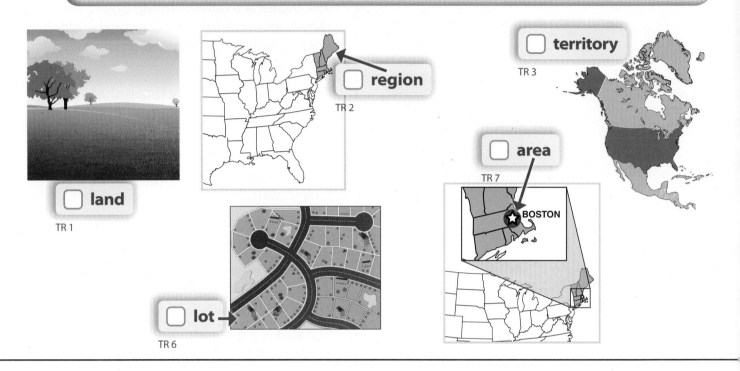

☐ **land**
TR 1

☐ **region**
TR 2

☐ **lot**
TR 6

☐ **territory**
TR 3

☐ **area**
TR 7

BOSTON

Check Your Understanding

A. Underline the correct word to complete each sentence.

1. Dad had a fence built to separate our (**lot / location**) from our neighbor's backyard.

2. Bill got a speeding ticket when he drove too fast through a construction (**territory / zone**).

3. Does France have any (**lots / territories**) in the Caribbean?

4. There are very good Japanese restaurants all throughout the Seattle (**area / location**).

5. Is there a (**place / territory**) where we can stop to rest?

6. My grandparents were farmers. They owned a lot of (**region / land**) for growing crops and raising animals.

7. When I called the police, they asked for my (**location / lot**).

8. Most of the southern (**region / lot**) of the United States has a warm climate.

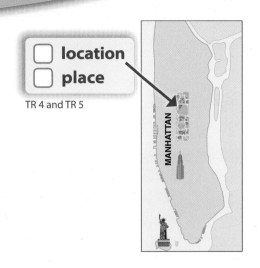

location
place

TR 4 and TR 5

MANHATTAN

zone

TR 8

Definitions

An **area** is a particular part of a town, a country, a region, or the world.

Land is an area of ground, especially one that is used for a particular purpose such as farming or building.

A **lot** is small area of land that belongs to a person or company.

A **location** is the place where something is.

A **place** is a particular building, area, town, or country.

A **region** is an area of a country or of the world.

Territory is all the land that a particular country owns.

A **zone** is an area marked for a special purpose.

B. Circle the correct example of each boldfaced word.

1. **land**	a. the ocean	b. a field	c. a table
2. **lot**	a. your yard	b. your car	c. your home
3. **place**	a. the beach	b. the ball	c. the phone
4. **region**	a. New York	b. England	c. the Southwest
5. **area**	a. a part of town	b. theater	c. corner
6. **location**	a. 412-555-2000	b. 505 Main Street	c. July 7, 2000
7. **territory**	a. neighbor's yard	b. shop	c. an area of land
8. **zone**	a. area surrounding a school	b. the front of the class	c. the teacher's desk

Challenge Words

Check (✔) the words you already know.

acre	frontier	premises	surface
domain	plot	site	terrain

265

139. Parks and Yards

Check (✔) the words you already know. Then, listen and repeat.

Tracks 1–6

☐ **patio**

TR 1

☐ **yard**

TR 2

☐ **park**

TR 3

Check Your Understanding

A. Match each word to the correct description. One description will not be used.

1. _____ schoolyard
2. _____ patio
3. _____ garden
4. _____ park
5. _____ yard
6. _____ playground

a. a public square in a city or town

b. an area outside of a school where children can play

c. a paved area found in a yard that normally has tables and chairs on it

d. an area with swings and slides for children to play on

e. a private area outside of a home with grass and trees

f. a public area with grass and trees

g. a place where flowers and vegetables are grown

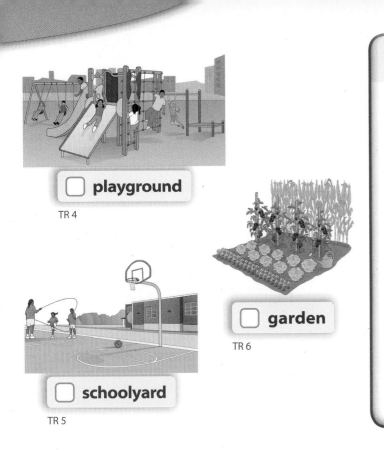

☐ playground
TR 4

☐ schoolyard
TR 5

☐ garden
TR 6

Definitions

A **garden** is a part of a yard where you grow flowers and vegetables.

A **park** is a public area of land with grass and trees where people exercise, play, or relax.

A **patio** is a paved area next to a house where people can sit and relax or eat.

A **playground** is a piece of land where children can play. **Playgrounds** often include equipment such as swings and slides.

A **schoolyard** is an area outside a school building where children play.

A **yard** is a piece of land next to a house, usually with grass and trees growing in it.

B. Choose the correct word from the word bank to complete each sentence. One word will not be used.

patio	yard	park	playground
garden	barnyard	schoolyard	

1. From the window, Julie can see her children playing on the grass in her _____ .

2. Are these tomatoes from your vegetable _____? They're delicious!

3. In the _____ in the center of town, there is a large, grassy area just for dogs.

4. It is so warm and pleasant this evening. Let's eat dinner out on the _____ .

5. The students are allowed to play in the _____ before and after classes.

6. I took my niece to the _____ and let her play on the swings.

Challenge Words

Check (✔) the words you already know.

☐ barnyard   ☐ cemetery   ☐ courtyard   ☐ plaza

267

168. Hills and Mountains

Check (✔) the words you already know. Then, listen and repeat.

Tracks 1–5

☐ **cliff**

TR 3

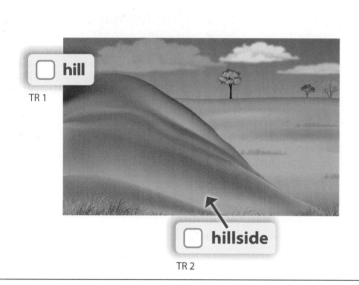

☐ **hill**

TR 1

☐ **hillside**

TR 2

Check Your Understanding

A. Circle the correct word or phrase to complete each sentence.

1. A _____ is an area of land that is higher than the land around it.

   a. hill   b. mound   c. hillside

2. Some people go to the _____ to climb them.

   a. mountains   b. hillsides   c. mounds

3. If I am standing at the edge of a _____ , I should be very careful not to fall.

   a. mound   b. cliff   c. hillside

4. The sloping part of a hill is called a _____ .

   a. hillside   b. cliff   c. mountain

5. Jorge created a _____ of dirt in his yard when he dug a hole.

   a. hillside   b. mound   c. cliff

☐ mound

TR 4

☐ mountain

TR 5

Definitions

A **cliff** is a high area of land with a very steep side.

A **hill** is an area of land that is higher than the land around it.

A **hillside** is the slope of a hill.

A **mound** of something is a rounded pile of it.

A **mountain** is a very high area of land with steep sides.

B. Choose the sentence that correctly uses the underlined word.

1. a. The doctor lives in the house on the <u>hill</u>.

   b. This <u>hill</u> is much taller than all the nearby mountains.

2. a. There is snow at the top of the <u>mountain</u>.

   b. The <u>mountain</u> is a flat, dry place that is always hot.

3. a. The kids are riding their bicycles up the <u>cliff</u>.

   b. The ocean waves are crashing into the <u>cliff</u>.

4. a. Let's walk down the <u>hillside</u> to get home.

   b. Let's go into the <u>hillside</u> to get out of the rain.

5. a. Did you see the <u>mound</u> of water in the park?

   b. Why is there a <u>mound</u> of dirt in your yard?

Challenge Words

Check (✔) the words you already know.

☐ crest   ☐ hilltop   ☐ mountaintop   ☐ slope

☐ dune   ☐ mountainside   ☐ plateau   ☐ volcano

267. Craters and Valleys

Check (✔) the words you already know. Then, listen and repeat.

Tracks 1–7

☐ **ditch**

TR 1

☐ **valley**

TR 2

☐ **pit**

TR 3

Check Your Understanding

A. Match each word to the correct description. One description will not be used.

1. _____ pit
2. _____ canyon
3. _____ valley
4. _____ manhole
5. _____ ditch
6. _____ hole
7. _____ crack

a. a deep, narrow hole next to a road

b. what you make in the ground when you dig

c. an underground passageway

d. an entrance for workers to go underground

e. a long valley with steep sides

f. a narrow gap that is often found in sidewalks

g. a low area between hills or mountains

h. an empty space

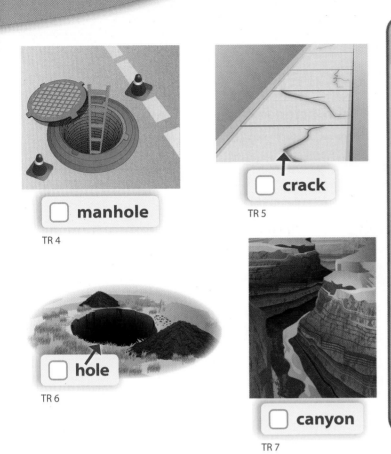

Definitions

A **canyon** is a long, narrow valley with very steep sides.

A **crack** is a very narrow gap between two things.

A **ditch** is a deep, long, narrow hole that carries water away from a road or a field.

A **hole** is an opening or an empty space in a surface.

A **manhole** is a hole in a road, usually covered by a metal lid, through which workers enter when they want to examine the pipes under the road.

A **pit** is a large hole that is dug in the ground.

A **valley** is a low area of land between hills and mountains.

B. Underline the correct word to complete each sentence.

1. From down in the (**manhole / canyon**), Victor could take beautiful photos of the surrounding mountains.

2. After the earthquake, the street was full of (**valleys / cracks**).

3. During the rainstorm, all the water flowed away from the road and into the (**ditch / canyon**).

4. Tom pulled the nail from the wall, leaving a (**pit / hole**).

5. Before they could plant the tree, my parents had to dig a small (**pit / canyon**).

6. I live in a low area between two mountains called Sunny (**Hole / Valley**).

7. When the water pipes broke, the workers had to go through the (**ditch / manhole**) to make the repair.

Challenge Words

Check (✔) the words you already know.

□ cavern   □ crater   □ gap   □ shaft

□ chasm   □ crevice   □ ravine   □ trench

271

362. Woodlands and Forests

Check (✔) the words you already know. Then, listen and repeat.

Tracks 1–2

☐ forest

TR 1

☐ jungle

TR 2

Definitions

A **forest** is a large area where trees grow close together.

A **jungle** is a forest in a tropical country where large numbers of tall trees and plants grow very close together.

Check Your Understanding

A. Write **T** for **true statements** and **F** for **false statements**.

1. _____ It is always hot and wet in a forest.

2. _____ A jungle is a kind of forest.

3. _____ Forests and jungles both have trees.

4. _____ Jungles are never in tropical countries.

B. Choose the best word from the word bank to complete each sentence. One word will be used two times. One word will not be used.

jungle	forest	thicket	forests

1. The boys went camping in the _____, and they were frightened when they saw a bear.

2. The rain that falls in the _____ helps the tropical plants grow.

3. My uncle works to protect the bears that live in the nearby _____ .

4. On our class trip to the _____, we were lucky to see several tropical birds.

Challenge Words

Check (✔) the words you already know.

☐ glade   ☐ grove   ☐ thicket   ☐ woodland

33 PLACES, LAND, AND TERRAIN

363. Pastures and Fields

Check (✔) the words you already know. Then, listen and repeat.

Tracks 1–2

☐ **field**

TR 1

☐ **prairie**

TR 2

Definitions

A **field** is a piece of land where crops are grown or where animals are kept.

A **prairie** is a large area of flat land in North America where very few trees grow.

Check Your Understanding

A. Circle the correct word to complete each sentence.

1. In a prairie, there are _____ .
   - a. very few trees
   - b. many hills
   - c. many people living close together

2. Fields can be used as a place for _____ .
   - a. keeping farm animals
   - b. growing vegetables
   - c. both *a* and *b*

3. Prairies are different from fields in that _____ .
   - a. prairies are generally larger than fields
   - b. prairies are very hilly areas
   - c. both *a* and *b*

B. Choose the sentence that correctly uses the underlined word.

1. a. That <u>field</u> is the best place in the city to find a parking spot.
   b. The farmer went to the <u>field</u> to see how the corn was growing.

2. a. Last summer we visited a <u>prairie</u> to learn about mountain climbing.
   b. It is easy to see across the <u>prairie</u> because it is so flat.

3. a. Near my grandmother's house in the country there is a <u>field</u> full of wildflowers.
   b. I like going to the <u>field</u> to see the ocean animals.

Challenge Words

Check (✔) the words you already know.

☐ battleground   ☐ meadow   ☐ paddy   ☐ vineyard

☐ countryside   ☐ orchard   ☐ pasture

398. Characteristics of Places

Check (✔) the word if you already know it. Then, listen and repeat.

Track 1

Definition

A **desert** is a very hot, dry, sandy area where little or no rain falls.

☐ **desert**

TR 1

Check Your Understanding

A. Write **T** for **true statements** and **F** for **false statements**.

1. _____ A desert is a dry place with little rain.

2. _____ It rains almost every day in the desert.

3. _____ A desert is a great place for growing crops.

B. Choose the sentence that correctly uses the underlined word.

1. a. Animals that live in the <u>desert</u>, such as camels, survive on very little water.

   b. John and I are planning to go swimming in the <u>desert</u>.

2. a. People that live in the <u>desert</u> have developed ways to live in very dry conditions.

   b. The <u>desert</u> was cold and there was a lot of snow on the ground.

3. a. John went to the <u>desert</u> on vacation, because he loved the hot weather and the sand.

   b. After dinner, I had a <u>desert</u> of ice cream.

Challenge Words

Check (✔) the words you already know.

☐ landscape   ☐ rural   ☐ urban

☐ mountainous   ☐ rustic   ☐ wilderness

78. Temperature

Check (✔) the words you already know. Then, listen and repeat.

Tracks 1–7

☐ **warm**

TR 1

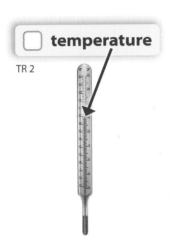

☐ **temperature**

TR 2

Definitions

A **chill** is a cold, but not freezing, temperature.

If someone or something is **cold**, it has a low temperature. A person may feel uncomfortable because they are not warm enough.

Someone or something that is **cool** has a low temperature, but is not cold.

Heat is warmth or the feeling of being hot.

Someone or something that is **hot** has a high degree of heat.

The **temperature** of something is how hot or cold it is.

Someone or something that is **warm** has some heat, but is not hot.

☐ **cool**

TR 3

☐ **heat**

TR 4

☐ **cold**

TR 7

☐ **chill**

TR 5

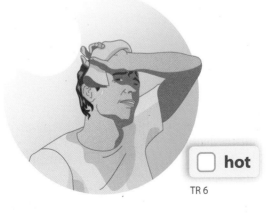

☐ **hot**

TR 6

Check Your Understanding

A. Circle the correct word to complete each sentence.

1. Today was a very _____ day. It was almost 100°.

   a. cool   b. heat   c. hot

2. After I exercise, I like to drink a _____ glass of water.

   a. temperature   b. cold   c. chill

3. Today's _____ will be fifty degrees.

   a. warm   b. cool   c. temperature

4. Do you have your jacket? There is a _____ in the air.

   a. chill   b. cold   c. heat

5. The family sat by the _____ fire after they came in from the snow.

   a. cold   b. warm   c. chill

6. The _____ outside is making me sweat.

   a. cold   b. heat   c. warm

7. It feels _____ under the tree, out of the sun.

   a. temperature   b. chill   c. cool

B. Underline the correct word to complete each sentence.

1. In the (**cold / hot**) weather, I usually wear my hat and gloves.

2. Tonight's low (**temperature / chill**) is twenty-five degrees.

3. I felt the (**heat / cool**) water before I jumped into the swimming pool.

4. Wrap yourself in this (**chill / warm**) blanket if you are cold.

5. During the winter, it is common to feel a (**chill / heat**) in the air.

6. Larry was sweating, so he opened a window in the (**cold / hot**) kitchen.

7. We sit near the fire to feel its (**chill / heat**).

Challenge Words

Check (✔) the words you already know.

☐ arctic   ☐ Fahrenheit   ☐ lukewarm   ☐ thermal
☐ Celsius   ☐ frigid   ☐ temperate   ☐ warmth

220. Fire

Check (✔) the words you already know. Then, listen and repeat.

Tracks 1–5

☐ **fire**

TR 1

Definitions

To **burn** something means to destroy or damage it with fire.

A **campfire** is a fire that you light outdoors when you are camping.

Fire is the hot, bright flames that come from things that are burning.

A **flame** is the bright burning gas that comes from a fire.

A **spark** is a hot flash or bit of light caused by fire.

☐ **burn**

TR 2

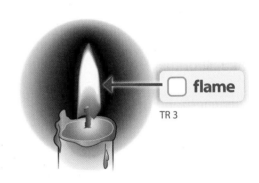

☐ **flame**

TR 3

☐ **spark**

TR 5

☐ **campfire**

TR 4

Check Your Understanding

A. Circle the correct words to complete the story.

My family went on a camping trip last weekend. We wanted to build a (1.) (**campfire / burn**) to cook dinner. However, we could not get the (2.) (**flame / fire**) started because we did not have any matches. My brother suggested that we rub sticks together. We did this for a very long time. Finally, a tiny (3.) (**campfire / spark**) came out from the sticks. We put some newspaper by the sparks, and it (4.) (**burned / fired**). Then, we added some wood. After a little while, there were many (5.) (**sparks / flames**). We cooked a nice dinner and were very proud of ourselves.

B. Match each word to the correct description. One description will not be used.

1. _____ fire
2. _____ burn
3. _____ campfire
4. _____ flame
5. _____ spark

a. to destroy or damage with fire

b. to start burning

c. hot, bright flames that come from something that is burning

d. a type of fire that you sit around when you are outside

e. bright burning gas

f. hot flash caused by fire

Challenge Words

Check (✔) the words you already know.

- ☐ blaze
- ☐ bonfire
- ☐ ignite
- ☐ singe
- ☐ sizzle
- ☐ smolder
- ☐ torch
- ☐ wildfire

376. Products of Fire

Check (✔) the words you already know. Then, listen and repeat.

Tracks 1–2

ash

TR 1

☐ smoke

TR 2

Definitions

Ash is the gray powder that remains after something has burned.

Smoke is the black, gray, or white clouds of gas that you see in the air when something burns.

Check Your Understanding

A. Write **T** for **true statements** and **F** for **false statements**.

1. _____ A fire can produce smoke and ash.

2. _____ It is not possible to see smoke.

3. _____ If you see smoke, there is probably a fire nearby.

4. _____ Normally a fire produces red and blue ashes.

B. Choose the correct word from the word bank to complete each sentence. Each word will be used twice.

ash	smoke

1. The thick, black _____ made it difficult to breathe.

2. After Clara burned the leaves, there was only _____ left.

3. Miguel could smell _____, so he knew a fire had started.

4. The fireplace was filled with gray _____ after the fire burned out.

Challenge Words

Check (✔) the words you already know.

☐ cinder   ☐ ember

414. Products Associated with Fire

Check (✔) the word if you already know it. Then, listen and repeat.

Track 1

☐ pipe

TR 1

Definition

A **pipe** is an object that is used for smoking tobacco.

Check Your Understanding

A. Write **T** for **true statements** and **F** for **false statements**.

1. _____ A pipe is a large tube of paper that some people smoke.

2. _____ A pipe is used for smoking.

3. _____ A pipe is made out of tobacco leaves.

B. Choose the sentence that correctly uses the underlined word.

1. a. The fireman used the <u>pipe</u> to put out the fire.

   b. It is not healthy to smoke a <u>pipe</u>.

2. a. Charlie's grandfather used to smoke a <u>pipe</u>, but then he quit.

   b. Melanie sat on the <u>pipe</u> and read a book.

3. a. People cannot smoke <u>pipes</u> inside the office.

   b. There is a <u>pipe</u> flying high in the sky.

Challenge Words

Check (✔) the words you already know.

☐ cigar   ☐ cigarette   ☐ tobacco   ☐ wick

131. Grabbing and Holding

Check (✔) the words you already know. Then, listen and repeat.

Tracks 1–10

☐ cuddle
TR 1

☐ snuggle
TR 2

☐ grab
TR 3

☐ hold
TR 4

☐ catch
TR 5

☐ pinch
TR 6

Definitions

To **catch** an object that is moving means to take hold of it with your hands.

To **clasp** someone or something means to hold on tightly.

To **cuddle** means to put your arms around a person and hold that person close.

To **grab** something means to take something quickly and roughly.

To **hold** something means to have it in your hands or arms.

To **hug** someone means to put your arms around that person.

When you **pick** flowers, fruit, or leaves, you take them from a plant or tree.

To **pinch** someone means to press that person's skin between your thumb and first finger.

To **snuggle** means to lie or sit close to someone in a loving way.

To **squeeze** means to press firmly, usually with your hands.

☐ squeeze
TR 7

☐ hug
TR 8

☐ clasp
TR 9

☐ pick
TR 10

Check Your Understanding

A. Choose the correct word from the word bank to complete each sentence. The first letter of each word is provided.

catch	hugs	clasped	grab	snuggle
holding	pick	cuddle	pinch	squeeze

1. Mary is **h** _____ Jennifer's purse while she puts her coat on.

2. To make lemonade, you must **s** _____ a lemon into a glass with sugar and water.

3. Tim went outside to **p** _____ some strawberries.

4. We like to **s** _____ with our dog and watch TV.

5. Carlos is going to **c** _____ the basketball and then pass it to Michael.

6. My mother **c** _____ my little brother's hand tightly as we crossed the street.

7. Luis **h** _____ his sister every time he says good-bye to her.

8. Alicia likes to **c** _____ with her kitten.

9. Ouch! That hurts! Why did you **p** _____ me?

10. Jeff was able to **g** _____ the dog before it ran away.

B. Underline the correct word to complete each sentence.

1. I (**grabbed / hugged**) my coat and ran out the door.

2. The apples are ready to eat, so we must (**pick / cuddle**) them soon.

3. Sue did not (**clasp / catch**) the ball, and her team lost the game.

4. When she was going down the stairs, my grandmother (**pinched / clasped**) the railing so she wouldn't lose her balance.

5. When Claire saw John sleeping, she (**pinched / hugged**) his arm to wake him up.

6. Rafaela (**picked / snuggled**) with the baby as he slept.

7. Sophia (**squeezed / picked**) four oranges so she could have fresh orange juice.

8. I (**catch / hug**) my mother to show that I love her.

9. It is difficult to (**grab / hold**) my dog because she is very heavy.

10. It's nice to (**cuddle / squeeze**) with someone you love.

Challenge Words

Check (✔) the words you already know.

☐ cling   ☐ embrace   ☐ grip   ☐ wrap

☐ clutch   ☐ grasp   ☐ pluck   ☐ wring

149. Specific Actions Done with the Hands

Check (✔) the words you already know. Then, listen and repeat.

 Tracks 1–5

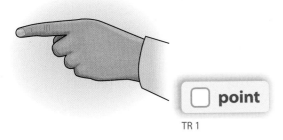

☐ **point**

TR 1

☐ **wave**

TR 2

Definitions

To **clap** means to hit your hands together, usually to show that you like something.

A **handshake** is a way people greet or leave each other, or agree on a decision, by grasping each other's hand.

When you **point**, you use your finger to show the direction of something.

To **salute** means to raise your hand, usually the right one, to your forehead to show respect or to honor someone.

To **wave** means to raise and move your hand from side to side, usually to say hello or good-bye.

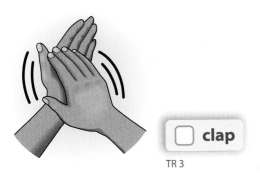

☐ **clap**

TR 3

☐ **salute**

TR 4

☐ **handshake**

TR 5

283

Check Your Understanding

A. Write the letter of the phrase that best completes each sentence.

1. _____ Bert gave a handshake to Ron . . .

   a. at the sailboat in the river.

2. _____ Julia waved good-bye to her mother . . .

   b. when they met for the first time.

3. _____ The soldiers saluted . . .

   c. as she left the house.

4. _____ The children clapped . . .

   d. at the end of the show.

5. _____ Freddy pointed . . .

   e. the army general to show respect.

B. Underline the correct word to complete each sentence.

1. Jon (**waved / pointed**) good-bye to his family before he got on the bus.

2. I greeted my new boss with a (**handshake / clap**).

3. The people (**saluted / clapped**) after the student finished her speech.

4. Jason (**pointed / handshake**) to an owl that he saw in the tree.

5. Soldiers usually (**salute / point**) when an important person, such as the president, walks by.

Challenge Words

Check (✔) the words you already know.

☐ fumble ☐ handiwork ☐ shrug ☐ wield

197. Feeling and Striking

Check (✔) the words you already know. Then, listen and repeat.

Tracks 1–13

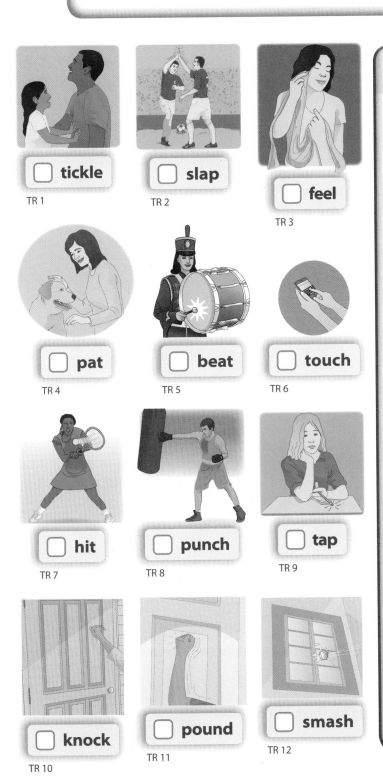

- ☐ tickle
  TR 1
- ☐ slap
  TR 2
- ☐ feel
  TR 3
- ☐ pat
  TR 4
- ☐ beat
  TR 5
- ☐ touch
  TR 6
- ☐ hit
  TR 7
- ☐ punch
  TR 8
- ☐ tap
  TR 9
- ☐ knock
  TR 10
- ☐ pound
  TR 11
- ☐ smash
  TR 12
- ☐ spank
  TR 13

Definitions

To **beat** something means to hit it very hard.

To **feel** something means to touch it with your hand so that you can find out what it is like.

To **hit** something means to touch it with a lot of force.

To **knock** on something means to hit it lightly in order to make a noise.

To **pat** something means to touch it lightly with the flat part of your hand.

To **pound** something means to hit it repeatedly with force.

To **punch** something means to hit it hard with a fist.

To **slap** something means to hit it with the flat inside part of your hand.

To **smash** something means to break it into many pieces with force.

To **spank** means to slap something with an open hand.

To **tap** something means to touch it quickly and lightly.

To **tickle** someone means to move your fingers lightly over a part of that person's body to make that person laugh.

To **touch** something means to put your hand onto it.

Check Your Understanding

A. Underline the correct word to complete each sentence.

1. In some countries, it is illegal to (**spank** / **knock**) children.

2. Angela (**punched** / **knocked**) on the door, but nobody answered.

3. It is important that you do not (**touch** / **smash**) the poisonous snake.

4. What does that blanket (**feel** / **pound**) like?

5. The baby laughed when his mother (**smashed** / **tickled**) his feet.

6. The firefighters (**patted** / **pounded**) on the door until someone opened it.

7. I (**tapped** / **slapped**) the bug when it landed on my arm.

8. During the storm, we could hear the rain (**feeling** / **beating**) down on the roof.

9. The baseball player (**patted** / **hit**) the ball over the fence.

10. Mrs. Sullivan asked us not to (**tap** / **spank**) our pencils against the desks during an exam.

11. Adam gently (**patted** / **punched**) his sister's hand to make her feel better.

12. The robbers used a hammer to (**feel** / **smash**) a window so that they could get in the house.

13. Bobby is in the principal's office because he (**tapped** / **punched**) another student in the arm.

B. Write **T** for **true statements** and **F** for **false statements**.

1. _____ If you hit a ball, you touch it with a lot of force.

2. _____ You use your fist to slap something.

3. _____ To spank means to move your fingers over a person's body to make them laugh.

4. _____ If you touch something, you put your hand on it.

5. _____ If you beat something, you gently touch it.

6. _____ You feel something with your hands to find out what it is like.

7. _____ When you knock on a door, you break it into small pieces.

8. _____ You use a lot of force to pat somebody on the hand or knee.

9. _____ If you pound on a drum, you hit it hard over and over again.

10. _____ You use a flat, open hand to punch something.

11. _____ If you smash a toy into little pieces, you might not be able to play with it again.

12. _____ If you tap something, you touch it quickly and lightly.

13. _____ Normally, people tickle children to make them upset.

Challenge Words

Check (✔) the words you already know.

☐ jab ☐ nudge ☐ smack ☐ stroke

☐ knead ☐ poke ☐ strike ☐ whack

APPENDIX

Note: This Appendix provides information on how to find each cluster. To locate a specific <u>super cluster</u>, please refer to the Contents on pages v to vi.

PHOTO CREDITS

Page 39: Mark Lund/Photodisc/Getty Images; nimblewit/Shutterstock.com; Picsfive, 2010/Used under; license from Shutterstock.com; eAlisa/Shutterstock.com; Scott Pehrson/Shutterstock.com; Smneedham/FoodPix/Getty Images

Pages 46–47: bonchan/Shutterstock.com; Brian A Jackson/Shutterstock.com; Louella938/Shutterstock.com; Joe Gough/Shutterstock.com; Josh Resnick/Shutterstock.com; Danny E Hooks/Shutterstock.com; Michael C. Gray/Shutterstock.com; Robyn Mackenzie/Shutterstock.com

Page 73: niderlander/Shutterstock.com; biletskiy/Shutterstock.com; Mircea; BEZERGHEANU/Shutterstock.com; Gregory Gerber/Shutterstock.com; Oliver Hoffmann/Shutterstock.com; Tobik/Shutterstock.com; Olga Lyubkina/Shutterstock.com

Page 105: Lebedinski Vladislav/Shutterstock.com; Ronald Sumners/Shutterstock.com; Tatiana Popova/Shutterstock.com; James Steidl/Shutterstock.com; Elena Schweitzer, 2010/Used under; license from Shutterstock.com; Sandra van der Steen/Shutterstock.com; sbarabu/Shutterstock.com

Page 123: Piotr Zajc/Shutterstock.com; Ekaterina Lin/Shutterstock.com; Aaron Amat/Shutterstock.com; Artmim/Shutterstock.com; Picsfive/Shutterstock.com; Ionia/Shutterstock.com

Page 152: Denis Kuvaev/Shutterstock.com; MaszaS/Shutterstock.com

Pages 156–157: Supri Suharjoto/Shutterstock.com; Edyta Pawlowska/Shutterstock.com; thefurnaceroom/iStockphoto.com; Meridian Studios/The Image Bank/Getty Images; Image Source/Getty Images

Page 177: James Thew/Shutterstock.com

Page 189: WilleeCole/Shutterstock.com; morrbyte/Shutterstock.com; Linda Armstrong/Shutterstock.com; Caitlin Mirra/Shutterstock.com; Just One Film/The Image Bank/Getty Images

Page 191: Mark Breck/Shutterstock.com; Richard Maschmeyer/Robert Harding World Imagery/Getty Images; Donald J. Price/Shutterstock.com; Flavio Coelho/Flickr/Getty Images; Oleg V. Ivanov/Shutterstock.com; trekandshoot/Shutterstock.com; SeanPavonePhoto/Shutterstock.com

Page 201: Photoroller/Shutterstock.com; leungchopan/Shutterstock.com

Page 206: Francesco Dazzi/Shutterstock.com

Page 207: Ruslan Semichev/Shutterstock.com; Verdateo/Shutterstock.com; VR Photos/Shutterstock.com; Lasse Kristensen/Shutterstock.com

Page 247: Nymph/Shutterstock.com; hartphotography/Shutterstock.com; Yuri Arcurs/Shutterstock.com; Monkey Business Images/Shutterstock.com; Gelpi/Shutterstock.com

Page 257: Andrew D. Bernstein/NBAE/Getty Images; Featureflash/Shutterstock.com

Page 263: Pola36/Shutterstock.com

Page 273: Elenamiv/Shutterstock.com; kavram/Shutterstock.com